HOLD

HOW TO FIND, BUY, AND RENT
HOUSES FOR WEALTH

HOW TO FIND, BUY, AND RENT
HOUSES FOR WEALTH

HOLD

STEVE CHADER, JENNICE DOTY, JIM McKISSACK, AND LINDA McKISSACK

WITH JAY PAPASAN

NEW YORK   CHICAGO   SAN FRANCISCO   LISBON   LONDON   MADRID   MEXICO CITY
MILAN   NEW DELHI   SAN JUAN   SEOUL   SINGAPORE   SYDNEY   TORONTO

ISBN: 978-0-07-179704-7
MHID: 0-07-179704-1

e-book ISBN: 978-0-07-179705-4
e-book MHID: 0-07-179705-X

McGraw-Hill books are available at special quantity discounts to use as premiums and sales promotions, or for use in corporate training programs. To contact a representative please e-mail us at bulksales@mcgraw-hill.com.

This book is printed on acid-free paper.

ACKNOWLEDGMENTS

The idea for this book was born back in 2004 when Gary, Dave, and I were still in the trenches writing its predecessor, *The Millionaire Real Estate Investor*. Little did we know how long the journey would be or how many people would contribute to these pages. Every book is the product of collaboration, some more so than others. *HOLD* took team writing to new heights. "Adventurous" may best describe the coordination of our creative book-writing process between four authors living in different towns, one contributing writer, four different content editors, as well as the large, talented support team that kept the train moving.

If you're reading these pages, chances are you contributed in some way and hope to find your name listed here. Should you not, please reach out. The responsibility rests squarely on my shoulders and the text will be amended to give you your rightful kudos. Likewise, I'll take ownership of any errors of fact or omission in the book itself; the expertise of the authors is unquestioned in our minds—surely any faults happened in the translation.

Speaking of the authors, a huge thanks to Jim and Linda McKissack, Jennice Doty, and Steve Chader for their generous and significant contributions of time and expertise over the years. This book would not exist without your determination and hard-won knowledge. In Gary's words, "You rock!"

Adding their thanks to my own, we'd like to thank the numerous people who helped bring *HOLD* to life. First and foremost Gary Keller, who continues to be a mentor and encourages us all to think big! To Mo Anderson, Mark Willis, Mary Tennant, and Jim Talbot, whose leadership and commitment to growing the wealth of others is inspiring.

Special thanks to writer Jolynn Rogers, who composed hours of interviews with all of the authors; editors Mark McFarlane and Jonas Koffler, who helped spearhead this project way back when; Katie Ford, who kept things moving in the right direction; Danny Thompson, who contributed his network and firsthand insights; übereditorial assistant Sarah Zimmerman, who did whatever it took to bring the manuscript to our standards and the finish line; Tamara Hurwitz and her production services team, specifically Mary Keith Trawick, who led the production, Jennifer Boyd, who headed the layout and design, Jeff Ryder and Justin McKinley, who comprised the copyedit and proofing team, and Brett Decker and Samantha Garza, for their continued and valuable support; Ellen Marks and her talented marketing team, specifically Hiliary Kolb and Annie Switt, Laura Price and Stephanie Van Hoek for championing the book to our readers, and Michael Balistreri and Caitlin McIntosh for their contributions to the cover design; and anchoring this section, the research team of Luke Smith, Kaitlin Merchant, Vickie Lukachik, and Kylah Magee, who earned our appreciation with tireless research and fact-checking.

We are grateful to a number of experts who freely gifted their know-how and expertise including Greg Sofio, David Reed, Gene Arant, Wendy Patton, Kenn Renner, David Greenberger, and J.P. Dahdah; and for Mary Glenn and her publishing team at McGraw-Hill for their continued partnership and support.

On a personal note, the authors would like to thank all of our family, friends, and colleagues. Without your unending support, we would not be where we are today! Thank you to Steve's wife Jill and two sons Matt and Chris; Jennice's parents Clayton and Patsy, husband Billy, sister Sheila, and other "sisters" Skeater, Brenda, and Sheila, and children Casey, Kirbi, and

Lane; Jim and Linda's family and children Beau, Melanie, Bailey, and Pres; Jesse Herfel, Bob Laird, the entire team at TCT Property Management Services, LLC, Natalie Effio, Erin Cowley (and sidekick Kristin), Beverly Steiner, Bruce Hardie, Erica Hill, Darrow Fiedler, Miki Nakajima, George Bliss, Brad and Susan McKissack and the McKissack Group in Denton, Texas, for helping us build a "business worth owning." Also thanks to our special friends who both support and inspire us: Gary and Nikki Ubaldini, Dianna Kokoszka and Tony DiCello, Mary and Joe Harker, Dr. Fred Grosse, Tony Jeary, Rob and Valerie Budd, Howard Brinton, STARS, and the many real estate agents around the United States and Canada who have been our teachers.

Finally, like the authors, I have to acknowledge that without the love and support of my wife and best friend Wendy, I wouldn't get very far at all. A successful real estate agent and investor herself, she manages our own investment portfolio and serves as my constant muse. Our kids Gus and Veronica deserve thanks too for living through this and our other entrepreneurial ventures. Playing "would you rather" on a road trip, our son asked, "Would you rather be stuck on an elevator for nine hours with dad talking about his books or mom talking to her clients?" Thanks for the laugh, Gus.

Jay Papasan
Vice President of Publishing and Executive Editor
Austin, Texas
August 1, 2012

CONTENTS

FOREWORD

I will never forget my first investment property. Why? It taught me one of the most important rules when it comes to real estate investing—cash flow is king.

It was 1984. I had just finished taking my first real estate investment class and was excited to apply what I had learned. So when a well-located condo came across my radar at a price point I could handle, I jumped. Six months later, the market dropped, the value of my investment plummeted. I saw several of my neighbors sell at foreclosure for about a third of the price I'd paid. But I couldn't afford to lose money—especially in year one.

So, I didn't. I held on.

Long story short, I held that property as an investment for sixteen years and never lost a cent. Month after month, year after year, the rental income was more than my expenses. In fact, not only did it continually cash flow, but once the market reemerged, the value had increased so much that I sold my first real estate investment for a terrific financial return.

The moral of the story is worth repeating: *cash flow is king*. As long as a property cash flows, it is a worthy and lucrative piece of your wealth-building portfolio that will lead you to financial freedom. This is such an important investment fact to remember, we actually thought about titling the book "Cash Flow."

The truth of the matter is money is everywhere. You just have to know where and how to look for it. You wouldn't step over a $100 bill on the sidewalk. Yet, most likely, you pass by thousand-dollar deals every day on your way to work or the gym or the grocery store.

HOLD will teach you how to spot the extra cash cleverly hidden in plain sight.

In 2005, we wrote the best-seller *The Millionaire Real Estate Investor* to provide an insider view on real estate being a rewarding place to invest your money. "Anyone can do it. Not everyone will ... will you?" was our slogan, and readers from all walks of life—stay-at-home moms, entrepreneurs, CEOs—got it, and wanted more.

Two years later, we partnered with Rick Villani and Clay Davis to write the best-seller *FLIP*. Rick and Clay were definitely it for the flip side of investing. At the time, they had more than fifteen years in personal real estate investment experience, plus over 1,000 flips with clients, and interested investors wanted to know how.

HOLD completes our investor trilogy by teaching you how to find, analyze, buy, manage, and grow investment properties long term for financial return. And, holding true to form, I thought, "Who better to cowrite with than people who have learned, lived, and perfected the HOLD strategy?"

Enter Steve Chader, Jennice Doty, and Jim and Linda McKissack.

Jim and Linda hit my radar in the early '90s, when they were looking to reinvent their financial futures. From day one, I knew they were destined to be successful investors. Their commitment, accelerated learning curve, and integrity were sure signs that I wanted to be in business with them.

In the same vein, I met Steve in the late '90s at a training event for top producers. He was one of a small, select group of real estate professionals who attended, and he stood out as not only a bright guy but, even more than that, a focused achiever. He quickly joined the leadership ranks among agents and continued to excel, independently finding outside talent to team up with. Welcome Jennice.

If there is one thing she knows, it is property management. Having worked as a longtime property manager, Jennice, at the time, had many years of behind-the-scenes, firsthand investment experience. Thankfully, she was able to learn her lessons watching others' mistakes. So, when the opportunity arose to partner with Steve in property management companies along with personal investments, her I spy goggles were already on.

Twenty-some years later, the four have morphed from pupils to professors in the classroom of wealth building. As their personal journeys have continued to grow, so has their passion for helping others begin their own tracks to financial freedom.

HOLD is more than a step-by-step strategy for increasing your wealth. It's a road map to building your financial future. And, Jim, Linda, Steve, and Jennice have more than paid their dues as HOLD experts through finding their own proven paths to financial freedom. If you follow the route they've plotted for you here, I know you too will be several steps farther on your wealth-building journey.

I want to personally congratulate you on buying this book. You are in great hands!

Gary Keller
Cofounder and Chairman of the Board
Keller Williams Realty, Inc.
www.KellerINK.com
July 21, 2012

INTRODUCTION

Ninety percent of all millionaires become so through owning real estate.

ANDREW CARNEGIE

TAKE HOLD OF YOUR FINANCIAL FUTURE

This book is more than a simple how-to guide. We want to challenge the way you view your role in personal wealth building. Of all the potential ways to grow wealth, we believe that buying and holding real estate is one of the most effective, reliable means to help fund a life of possibilities that each of us deserves. It requires less capital and offers more control to the investor than most other forms of investing.

HOLD is not about getting rich quick; we'll leave that to the late-night infomercials. This book will be your guide to a proven, reliable real estate investing process (Find, Analyze, Buy, Manage, and Grow). The HOLD strategy is not about gambling for a big payday but rather about building a stable foundation to build your net worth and deliver consistent cash flow over time. Like anything that offers meaningful rewards, you will have to work. But it's not a full-time job, and it won't steal your free time. It doesn't require an MBA, but it will improve your financial smarts. It's a worthwhile journey, and with this book you're on your way!

We all work toward a future vision of financial freedom. Our parents did it, as did their parents before them. What's changed is what the path to that end goal might look like. In the past, it looked something like this: Get a good job with a good company that will provide a sizable pension to live off of after age 65. And Social Security? Well, that's just an added bonus.

Today, that journey is not cut from the same cloth—or even a good knockoff. Rather, the average person will change jobs nine to thirteen times during a career, which means bye-bye pension plan. Already more than half of working Americans do not expect to look to government funding like Social Security when the "golden years" come knocking. So, it's no surprise that aside from playing the stock market or starting a small business, many—like you—are looking to invest their future security in real estate.

From Debt to Riches: The Story of Jim and Linda McKissack

Launching a long-standing career in real estate investing was not what Jim and Linda McKissack had in mind when they bought their first investment property in 1991. Only four years earlier, Jim had boarded up his Dallas nightclub, which left the couple more than $600,000 in debt. To offset the loss, Linda took a job in real estate sales, and Jim went to work in her office. He also met with his bankers to structure a repayment plan. It was simply a means to get them back in the black—and it worked. Together, the couple put all of their money into settling debts.

With their debt satisfied, the McKissacks decided to invest in another piece of real estate. Luckily, timing found them. After the savings and loan crisis of the 1980s, many properties were foreclosed, and it was a buyer's market for sure. Jim and Linda found a run-down property held by the Resolution Trust Corporation (RTC). With the help of a local builder, they bought and rehabilitated the property. After flipping it for a small profit, they bought another RTC property: a two-story house in their town's historical district. The couple bought the property for $15,000 and then spent another $60,000 to repair the house and convert it to a fourplex. This time, they held onto the property, filled the building with tenants, and began receiving a steady cash flow of rent. That fourplex began their career as HOLD real estate investors.

As their cash flow grew, Jim and Linda started saving 15 percent of every real estate sales commission check in a money market account. Whenever the account reached $15,000 to $20,000, they would use it for a down payment on another property, financing it for fifteen years. In the beginning, their goal was to purchase two properties a year. Encouraged by their success, they accelerated their savings by growing Linda's real estate business and keeping their life small. Before long, however, they were buying 15 to 20 properties a year, as long as each property met their purchasing criteria. At one time, the McKissacks owned more than 100 residential properties alone.

Jim and Linda now head a real estate enterprise that encompasses 79 single-family homes, 6 commercial buildings, 2 multifamily structures, 6 vacation rental cabins, and 5 real estate franchises in Texas, Indiana, and Ohio, all with an annual cash flow of more than $1 million.

And that fourplex that kicked off their HOLD journey? It's still in their portfolio and generating a steady $3,000 a month in cash flow.

Build a Business Worth Owning: The Story of Steve Chader and Jennice Doty

Steve Chader remembers when he was a boy, sitting at the table with his grandfather, Kolin Hager. His grandfather looked up from the newspaper he was reading and uttered these words of advice: "Buy stocks in great companies like RCA."

A pioneer in radio and the general manager of station WGY in Albany, New York, Steve's grandfather felt confident recommending RCA, which everyone at the time viewed as an innovative powerhouse of a company with a limitless future. But by the time Steve was old enough to think about investing, RCA was gone.

Fast forward a few years to when Steve moved west to complete a degree in distribution and transportation at Arizona State University in the city of Mesa. It was the late 1970s, and people and companies were leaving New York in droves to escape rising taxes.

Steve noticed all the new houses being built in Mesa and the rising property values there. He felt the city was on the verge of something big, and he decided to be a part of it. After graduating from college, Steve stayed there and began selling real estate. He called his father back home.

"You won't believe what's happening here: property values are going up, and you can get positive cash flow on rents," Steve told his dad, who decided to loan Steve the money to buy a duplex (a foreclosure) in exchange for a share of the profits.

Steve and his new wife, Jill, lived in one side of the duplex, rented out the other side, and managed the property. His monthly payment turned out to be less than the rent he was paying for his apartment. Steve's grandfather became his next investor. Instead of the 3 percent to 4 percent in interest his grandfather was getting from his CD investment, Steve paid his grandfather 9 percent.

That was the beginning. With his first two investments doing well, Steve started calling friends back on the East Coast, convincing them to buy duplexes in Mesa that he would manage for a fee. As his success grew and he continued to buy and sell property, real estate investing became like a game of Monopoly. Just like the board game, Steve was steadily building wealth by buying less-expensive properties and trading up to larger properties and commercial investments.

In 1993, Jennice Doty started working for Steve as a part-time property manager. Jennice had a background managing office buildings and retail complexes, but she never thought of becoming an investor. Her mindset soon changed.

Over the years, Jennice helped Steve more than quadruple the business—not only by growing their property management services, but also by being an investment partner. Today, the pair own 9 single-family properties and 5 commercial buildings in the Phoenix area, and manage approximately 1,000 residential and 40 commercial properties.

WHAT CAN THE HOLD STRATEGY DO FOR YOU?

Learning and living the HOLD approach can help you build your wealth and realize your future financial goals too. The authors' stories get to the heart of what makes real estate such a great investment. As President Franklin Roosevelt once declared: "Real estate cannot be lost or stolen, nor can it be carried away. Purchased with common sense, paid for in full, and managed with reasonable care, it is about the safest investment in the world."

With an emphasis on "purchased with common sense," we believe it can be not only the safest, but also one of the best investments you can make. HOLD will show you how to purchase it, pay for it, and manage it, as Roosevelt instructed.

Once you see what the HOLD strategy can do for you, you may find yourself—like the four coauthors of this book—sharing your knowledge with employees, friends, and others who want to add this real estate investment model to their own portfolio. As Linda puts it: "We've seen the difference it has made in our lives, so when we see other people struggling and facing challenges, we want them to try it too because we know it works."

OVERVIEW

HOLD: THE ULTIMATE WEALTH-BUILDING STRATEGY

1. FIND
The right property for the right terms and the right price

Outcome: a list of qualified investment properties from which to choose

2. ANALYZE
A property to make sure the numbers and the terms make sense

Outcome: a prospect that meets your financial criteria

3. BUY
An investment property where you make money going in

Outcome: a profitable property to add to your HOLD investment portfolio

4. MANAGE
Your tenants and properties like a pro

Outcome: a sustainable investment property for your HOLD portfolio

5. GROW
Your way to wealth and financial freedom

Outcome: an investment portfolio that funds the life you want to live

Figure O-1

HOLD is a long-term real estate investment strategy to which every real estate investor should aspire to follow. With this method, you can "buy it right" from the beginning and grow your investment portfolio over a longer, historically more stable and predictable time period.

The HOLD strategy consists of five key elements: Find, Analyze, Buy, Manage, and Grow. We'll examine each of these elements in greater depth in the following chapters of this book. But, for now, we'll describe how each one plays a part in achieving maximum appreciation and cash flow growth.

> **Find**: The search is on for a great real estate investment that minimizes risk and maximizes financial returns. The secret lies in having the right criteria based on the underlying fundamentals of price, terms, and condition. It truly is a numbers game. You'll learn to be a master at defining financial criteria that make a real estate investment work. Find isn't about looking for opportunity that isn't there, but rather identifying prospects available in any market and having the systems in place to respond without hesitation when the right opportunity presents itself.

> **Analyze**: Careful analysis is what enables you to eliminate poor investments and recognize a great deal among a handful of good ones. If you do your due diligence rightly and routinely, using well-supported evidence of current market values, rents, and home price appreciation, you will limit your risk significantly. Throughout this section, you'll rely on our HOLD Property Analysis Worksheet to guide you through each step of the process, collect the relevant

numbers, and make critical calculations. During analysis set your emotions aside. The numbers must meet your criteria or there is no reason to buy!

Buy: This is when you make the first investment in your HOLD portfolio. If you have the right numbers, you'll make money on the margin and achieve positive cash flow from the start. A cardinal rule is not to buy a property hoping it will appreciate and become a good deal; you buy because it's already a good deal. The successful investor always makes her money going in.

Manage: Let the wealth building begin! Professional property managers have proven systems for every aspect of HOLD ownership. This is where you'll learn how to lease properties, manage tenants, handle maintenance and repairs, as well as stay on top of your budget and recordkeeping. In short, you'll learn how to run your investment properties like a business.

Grow: If one investment property can strengthen your financial position, just imagine how a portfolio of cash-flowing properties can change your life. The HOLD real estate strategy is an endless and participatory opportunity loop in which you're constantly finding, analyzing, buying, managing, and growing your real estate portfolio. As long as you are purposeful about this strategy and let the fundamentals work in your favor, you'll leverage your way to wealth and financial freedom—faster than you might think.

HOLD'S RETURN ON INVESTMENT

Real estate is a tangible asset like gold or silver. No matter what might happen to the structure, you still own the land underneath. And much like gold or silver, real estate tends to appreciate in value, yielding a dependable financial return over time. Funny thing is when you start talking money with experienced investors, the terminology changes. Experts talk in rules of thumb—rent-to-price ratios, cap rates, and cash-on-cash returns. But, they've also earned this right after years of experience building portfolio after portfolio. These shortcuts are useful and have their place, but they should never replace the fundamentals we'll teach you in "Analyze" for making a purchase decision.

With *HOLD* we'll avoid the jargon and keep things simple. First, return on investment (ROI) is the same thing as rate of return (ROR). Second, we're going to talk cash flow, meaning your income after all expenses including taxes, operating costs, and mortgage payments. This differs from your net operating income (NOI), which refers to your total income after all expenses, *not* including your mortgage. We realize commercial investors interchange the two, but that is because often properties in that realm are bought in cash and have no mortgage to account for. Here, for all intents and purposes:

Net Operating Income − Debt Service = Cash Flow

Or, in plain English: Your monthly cash flow is your monthly rent income minus all monthly expenses including your mortgage payment (debt service). If this all still seems clear as mud, fear not. You'll be financially fluent in no time.

Now that we have the HOLD speak set, let's look at three financial returns you can depend on using this strategy:

1. **Cash Flow**. As we said, this is the total amount of money remaining after all expenditures are paid including taxes, operating costs, and mortgage payments. It is the most direct type of financial return, because it's money you put in your pocket every month, and it provides you with the working capital to expand your investment opportunities.

2. **Pay Down**. This HOLD strategy gives you the power of leverage. With every mortgage payment, you're decreasing your debt and building equity in your investment simultaneously. Better yet, you're not even the one paying down the debt! Each time your tenants pay the rent, they are building equity for you. So, regardless of appreciation rates, if a property generates a cash flow, you continue to benefit. Your debts are being paid down, meaning your equity remains on the steady climb. Meanwhile, you keep adding extra green to your pockets.

3. **Appreciation**. This is a second way you build up equity, and it can be your greatest financial return using the HOLD model because, historically, real estate has reliably increased in value over time—through inflation and supply and demand. However, this rate is not fixed, so there is no guaranteed appreciation on an annual basis. It's important too to remember that a national average will not always reflect your local market's appreciation rates. For the purposes of this book, we are going to go middle of the road and use an annual appreciation return of 4.4 percent, which according to the U.S. Census Bureau and National

Association of Realtors is the median from 1970 to 2010, and includes three housing downturns. It's possible to achieve far greater rates of price appreciation, but we believe that this is the icing on the cake. Cash flow and debt pay down are the primary drivers wise investors base their financial plans on. Let's take a closer look.

Watch the Three Drivers of Real Estate Investment at Work

Say you buy a single-family home listed at $170,000. Because you worked hard to find a deal, you negotiate a price of purchase for $153,000—a 10 percent discount. Using conventional financing, you put down 25 percent; $38,250—on a 30-year note. Your mortgage principal is $114,750; that's your purchase price minus your down payment. We're going to walk you through a hypothetical but realistic scenario to illustrate how your cash flow, debt pay down, and appreciation drive your financial returns individually and collectively and, trust us, it only gets better from there.

List Price: $170,000

10% Discount: $17,000

Purchase Price: $153,000

25% Down Payment: $38,250

Mortgage: $114,750 on a 30-Year Note

Figure O-2

Aim for immediate cash flow

As we said earlier, cash flow is king, and you successfully bought a property that will generate a monthly cash flow of $100 after debt service and expenses. As you can see in figure 0-3, based on your actual down payment of $38,250, you have slightly better than a 3 percent return rate on cash flow, or $1,200 in year one. Three percent may not seem like much, but remember, this is only the beginning.

The Power of Cash Flow in Year One	
Annual Cash Flow	$1,200
Rate of Return on Cash Flow	3.1%

Figure 0-3

Track debt pay down

Aside from cash flow, appreciation is the measuring stick most people look to when tracking a property's return on investment. But what many don't realize is the importance of debt pay down. He's our unsung hero because not only does your equity build and rate of return go up as you pay down your debt, but your tenants are actually paying it down for you. Double whammy. As you can see in figure 0-4, your annual debt pay down is $1,179, which is also slightly better than a 3 percent return on your investment. And, when cash flow and debt pay down are combined, you're already topping a

6 percent financial return. And that's with zero appreciation. Oh, and by the way, in the first year your tenants paid $7,927 in interest on your mortgage, as well.

The Power of Debt Pay Down in Year One	
Annual Debt Pay Down	$1,179
Annual Cash Flow	$1,200
Total Return	**$2,379**
Rate of Return on Cash Flow	3.1%
Rate of Return on Debt Pay Down	3.1%
Rate of Return on Total	6.2%

Figure 0-4

Appreciate the add-on of appreciation

It's great to build a solid rate of return without appreciation, but who doesn't love icing on a cupcake? That's the added bonus of appreciation. It does vary from year to year and location to location, but it is usually a sweet bonus. As you can see in figure 0-5, we are using the 30-year median appreciation rate of 4.4 percent again, or in this case $7,480—which alone represents a 19.5 percent return on investment. When you add the three drivers together, your property is returning more than 25 percent in year one. And those numbers don't even factor in the $17,000 discount you earned by finding and negotiating a great deal. What other investment strategy yields these numbers?

The Power of Appreciation in Year One	
Annual Debt Pay Down	$1,179
Annual Cash Flow	$1,200
Annual Appreciation	$7,480
Total Return	**$9,859**
Rate of Return on Cash Flow	3.1%
Rate of Return on Debt Pay Down	3.1%
Rate of Return on Appreciation	19.5%
Rate of Return on Total	**25.7%**

Figure 0-5

And, as an added bonus, there are often tax benefits to investing in real estate in the United States and Canada—depreciation deductions, no capital gains tax until the property is sold. Governments offer these incentives as a way to encourage and support real estate investment, which is a pillar of a healthy national economy. However, they are by no means fixed rates of return, so it's important to consult a tax adviser and never invest in a property strictly for tax benefits.

LEARN THE LEVERAGE HABIT

One of the biggest advantages to real estate investing is that you don't have to go it alone. You can leverage money, people, and time *to help you build your personal wealth*.

To understand the leverage habit, start by thinking of the root word of leverage, which is *lever*. A lever is a simple tool that can multiply the mechanical force you apply to an object. With a lever, you can accomplish more than would be possible on your own. As the Greek mathematician and inventor Archimedes once said: "Give me a lever long enough and a fulcrum on which to place it, and I shall move the world."

Leverage Money

We don't know of another investment opportunity that you can buy at 25 percent down at a fixed interest rate over 15 to 30 years. While you can borrow money for stocks by buying them on margin, that's a niche strategy used mainly in short-term investments.

In real estate investing, the opposite is true. By putting down only 25 percent, you can own a $170,000 asset that appreciates a historical average of 4.4 percent annually, bringing its value to $177,480 in one year. When you weigh your $38,250 investment against a 4.4 percent gain, it translates to a 19.5 percent rate of return.

The Power of Leverage on Rate of Return	
Fair Market Value	$170,000
Purchase Price	$153,000
Down Payment	$38,250
Appreciation (1 Year @ 4.4%)	$7,480 ($170,000 x 4.4%)
Rate of Return on Price	4.4% ($7,480 / $170,000)
Rate of Return on Investment	19.5% ($7,480 / $38,250)

Figure O-6

And if you buy at a discount, as we did in the previous example, your money will work even harder for you. You also can borrow against your equity by securing a second loan or refinancing the original loan plus the increased equity—converting any equity gains into cash without selling the asset. Then you can use the cash to fund other investments. That's the magic of leveraging your money in real estate.

Leverage People

The longer we're in this business, the more we understand that we can't do this alone. Relationships are the lifeblood of successful real estate investing. Whether it's a relationship with a bank, plumber, or real estate agent, a solid network of professionals can make your life easier and more profitable. And, it's important to establish that network early.

That's why we say that before you purchase your first piece of property, you need to put together your investment team. By that, we mean a team of professionals who understand your investment strategy and are dedicated to helping you achieve your goals. Your team should include the following:

- **A real estate agent**. The first person you need on your team is a real estate agent, preferably one who's familiar with real estate investing and understands the goals of your real estate investment strategy. For your first property, find an agent you trust who shares a similar philosophy to your investment strategy. That way, he or she will be able to recognize a good deal for you. Also, real estate agents with long histories of buying and selling investment properties are great resources for finding other professionals who can serve on your investment team. They know who the best people are and how to contact them. That's why they come first.

- **A lender**. Having a knowledgeable lender is vital, because he or she will help you set the terms and conditions that can make or break a real estate deal. There are advantages to working with local lending institutions and with national banks. Smaller banks can be conducive to fostering more personal working relationships, which can come in handy over the years as you're managing your HOLD investments. However, national banks often have access to more capital and competitive pricing. In the end, it always pays to do business with a lender who has extensive experience handling real estate investments.

Also important to consider is that every bank has a niche. Some banks specialize in lending to small businesses, others deal heavily in commercial real estate transactions, while still others specialize in construction loans. Ask other investors to find the banks that specialize in your type of real estate transactions.

- **A property manager**. A good property manager is more than a rent collector or a part-time real estate agent. You want one who does property management full time. Many professional property managers choose to focus on the needs of the investor, and they don't get distracted by listing and selling property. Look for someone who returns phone calls promptly and knows how to turn your property around quickly. No more than three days should pass between a tenant moving out and your property being ready for the next renter. Good property managers are worth their weight in gold.

They can maximize your rental revenues, help you assess whether or not to buy a property, and give you advice about insurance coverage, landlord/tenant laws, and government requirements. Talk to other investors to get referrals or contact your local real estate board. They'll know which property managers are getting kudos and which ones are getting complaints.

- **An attorney**. Find an attorney who knows how to do real estate transactions and—for a reasonable price—can establish business entities, such as a limited liability company or partnership. You can find these attorneys by networking with other investors and seeing which ones in your area are accustomed to handling a variety of complicated real estate transactions. You wouldn't hire a real estate attorney to handle your divorce, nor should you have a divorce attorney handling your real estate transactions.

- **A certified public accountant**. There's a difference between a CPA who crunches numbers for taxes and one who understands the tax implications of real estate. Our advice is to find a CPA knowledgeable in real estate and meet with her quarterly, especially before your tax returns are due to make sure you have taken all your deductions. If your CPA is philosophically in tune with real estate as *the* method for building wealth, you'll find this is money well spent.

While these professionals play critical roles on your HOLD investment team, they certainly aren't the only experts you can leverage along the way. Over the years, you'll develop an even wider network of repairmen and trade professionals—all of whom can help you bring out the best in your HOLD investment portfolio.

Figure O-7

Give your team vision

The first rule in putting together your investment team is that each of the members needs to understand your investment goals and vision. Let's say your goal is to be financially independent in fifteen years. Everybody on the team needs to know what that means. Define it. If you want a real estate portfolio that generates $100,000 in after-tax cash flow in fifteen years, then that is your goal. Once you choose your teammates, you need to consult with them as early in the process as possible so you can benefit from their expertise. Your real estate agent will do a "needs analysis," find out what you're trying to achieve, and then go out and find deals that match your criteria. Your accountant and attorney can advise you on legal and tax implications *before* you find a deal, so that you can avoid potential problems.

The point is to leverage their time, talent, and wisdom, as well as their contacts, to help you achieve your goals faster and more efficiently than you would on your own.

A second way to leverage people using the HOLD strategy is to reach out to individuals who are already successful. Find the knowledge leaders in the industry, and ask them how they got started and what their aha's have been. Learning from an experienced investor will save you time and money, and teach you things that otherwise might have taken you years to discover. If you don't know anybody in the business, reach out to real estate agents or attend a real estate investing club meeting in your area.

Look at it this way: Instead of asking yourself, "What do I need to do?" Ask yourself, "Who can I talk to? Who knows how to do this?" The stakes in real estate investing can be high. There is no reason to learn from your mistakes when you can avoid them by consulting with others who have been there before. As soon as you change the question from what to who, you'll be surprised how many people show up to help.

Leverage Time

Whether you're young or old, it's smart to leverage time. Many would-be investors never get past the starting gate because they think they don't have the time, or they overestimate the time it will take. The HOLD strategy of buying and holding rental property is the ultimate way to leverage time because while you're working at your job, your investments are working for you.

Albert Einstein is often cited as the proof that we should give compound interest more respect. For well over fifty years, quotes like: "Compound interest is the eighth wonder of the world," and "Compound interest is the most powerful force in the universe" have been attributed to the Nobel prize-winning scientist by everyone from weekend blog-gers to presidential speech writers. Einstein probably never said or wrote anything of the sort, but it doesn't make the statement false. Interest is accrued income on a principal amount. Compound interest is additional income amassed off of that interest, and it has the power to astound.

But, as you can imagine, it's hard to calculate. While Einstein may have been able to do the mental math on how long it would take for your $170,000 investment property to double in value if home prices appreciated at a historical rate of 4.4 percent, the rest of us need help. That's why we love the Rule of 72.

Follow the Rule of 72

Charlie Munger, vice chairman of Berkshire Hathaway and well-known investor, pointed to the Rule of 72 with partner Warren Buffett as one of the key "mental models" to know in investing. Though not exact, the Rule of 72 allows investors to quickly guesstimate how long it will take for their investment to double in value given various return rates. So how does it work? Let's walk through an example.

Say you want to know how many years it would take to double your investment with a 4.4 percent appreciation rate. Divide 72 by 4.4 and you get about 16.4 years. Figure 0-8 illustrates a larger range of estimates vs. actuals using the Rule of 72 at varying return rates. We tell investors a great target for a total return (cash flow, debt pay down, and appreciation) is 17 to 20 percent in real estate. You can do better, but in this range, you know your money is really working for you. You double your money almost every four years.

Rule of 72 Formula Analysis			
Rate of Return	Actual Years to Double	Rule of 72 Estimate	Time Difference
2%	35.0	36.0	1.0
3%	23.4	24.0	0.6
5%	14.2	14.4	0.2
6%	11.9	12.0	0.1
7%	10.2	10.3	0.0
9%	8.0	8.0	0.0
12%	6.1	6.0	-0.1
15%	5.0	4.8	-0.2
17%	4.4	4.2	-0.2
20%	3.8	3.6	-0.2
25%	3.1	2.9	-0.2
50%	1.7	1.4	-0.3
72%	1.3	1.0	-0.3

Figure 0-8

The Rule of 72 is a good example of leveraging time. No matter your current situation or how little money or time you have in the beginning, you can get where you want to go. All you have to do is start. After all, the longest journeys are an accumulation of small steps.

None of the authors of this book started out imagining they would build the real estate portfolios they own today. Each of them started small, and through the magic of leverage over time, they far exceeded whatever dreams they once imagined.

POINTS TO REMEMBER

HOLD is a long-term investment strategy for those who want to build financial wealth through real estate. It yields long-term cash flow and equity buildup.

You know you are ready to follow the HOLD strategy when you:

- Establish personal wealth-building goals for your future.

- Actively explore real estate wealth building.

- Save for a down payment and reserve fund.

- Assemble a group of professionals to set a plan of action.

STAGE 1: FIND

> ## 1. FIND
> **The right property for the right terms and the right price**
>
> ☐ **Chapter 1**: Create Your Personal Investment Criteria
>
> ☐ **Chapter 2**: Create Your Property Criteria
>
> ☐ **Chapter 3**: Lead Generate for Properties

Outcome: a list of qualified investment properties from which to choose

You got to be careful if you don't know where you're going, because you might not get there.

YOGI BERRA

Now that you have seen the benefits of the HOLD strategy, it's time to go out and find a house to buy. Sounds simple, right? Everywhere you look there are houses for sale. But, as with any discipline, there's an art to finding the right house for your investment goals.

Like a prospector panning for gold or a wildcatter looking for oil, you can waste a lot of time and money if you charge ahead without a plan. The lack of a plan is probably the biggest mistake new investors make. They buy a house because they *feel* it's a good deal, vs. *knowing* it's a good investment. You have a much greater chance of reaching your goals faster—and with much less risk—if you pick your investment model, build your criteria, and then find properties that fit your criteria. It's ready, *aim*, fire.

Don't think of real estate investing as a one time transaction; think of it as part of your long-term wealth building strategy. You need to have your approach in place before you make a move, and then periodically review your plan to ensure it continues to support your financial goals.

In this section, you'll learn how to develop personal and property criteria that will help you identify investment opportunities that support your financial objectives. You'll also learn how and where to find the best potential HOLD properties and how to rally the support of others who can help you meet your investment goals. Let's get started!

CHAPTER 1:
CREATE YOUR PERSONAL INVESTMENT CRITERIA

1. FIND
The right property for the right terms and the right price

- ☐ **Chapter 1**: Create Your Personal Investment Criteria
- ☐ **Chapter 2**: Create Your Property Criteria
- ☐ **Chapter 3**: Lead Generate for Properties

Outcome: a list of qualified investment properties from which to choose

After reading this chapter, you will know how to:

☐ Define your HOLD mission and vision.

☐ Determine your preferred time frame, rate of return, and risk tolerance.

☐ Understand the importance of a wealth adviser.

FOCUS YOUR MISSION FOR A CLEAR VISION

You are the head of your investment portfolio. And, as any good leader must do, it's up to you to define the mission—"where are we going?"—and vision—"how will we know when we get there?"—for your investment team. In other words, before you decide *what* to buy, you need to understand *why* you are investing in real estate. The HOLD strategy focuses on two primary financial drivers to determine investors' property criteria: cash flow and net worth.

Depending on where you are in your financial journey, your criteria may be very different. If you are a twenty-eight-year-old single female aiming to purchase your first home as an investment property, your personal investment criteria probably looks nothing like a couple in their fifties looking for a property portfolio that will afford them retirement in ten years.

For example, let's go back to the $170,000 single-family home you bought at a 10 percent discount in the previous section. In that scenario, you purchased on a 30-year note and in year one enjoyed total financial returns of about $9,859—a rate of return more than 25 percent of your initial investment—and cash flow of $1,200 from the get-go. What happens when you HOLD that property for thirty years and pay it off completely? In year thirty, your property would be cash flowing $17,908 annually, and would have cash flowed nearly a quarter of a million dollars over its lifetime. Your accumulated financial return would be $812,387, and you'd be turning the corner toward $1 million.

Now, if you rewind again, and buy the same property on a 15-year note, what do you think those same numbers look like? It may be surprising that your investment would have negative cash flow until year six. The same rent that generated $100 in monthly cash flow on a 30-year note won't initially cover the higher monthly note on a 15-year mortgage. But, at the thirty-year mark, the property would have been paid off for fifteen years, cash flowing $27,014 annually and would have produced an accumulated cash flow of more than $340,000. Your property's accumulated financial return on investment in year thirty would be $905,065.

YEAR	ANNUAL CASH FLOW		ACCUMULATED CASH FLOW		ACCUMULATED FINANCIAL RETURN ON INVESTMENT	
	30 year	15 Year	30 year	15 Year	30 year	15 Year
1	$1,200	-$1,727	$1,200	-$1,727	$9,859	$10,408
6	$3,076	$149	$12,705	-$4,858	$71,291	$78,348
15	$7,335	$4,408	$60,757	$16,849	$245,075	$285,906
30	$17,908	$27,014	$248,960	$341,639	$812,387	$905,065

30-Year vs. 15-Year: How Notes Affect Cash Worth

Figure 1-1

As you can see in figure 1-1, both scenarios prove large financial returns, but each has its own path to get there. The 30-year model immediately cash flows and can be used as a reliable source of income year over year. The 15-year model, on the other hand, has apparent up-front risk, as it does not cash flow until year six. However, if you can afford to put money in for five years with no cash flow, you will reap higher financial returns more quickly as you rapidly pay down the mortgage principal and increase equity.

Of course, it is important to remember this is a hypothetical scenario. The main purpose of showing you the side-by-side comparison on this property is to illustrate how different approaches play out. For the record, we do not advise buying an investment property that does not cash flow—and definitely not one that isn't cash flowing until year six.

Let's take a look at some real-life scenarios.

Increase Your Cash Flow

Again, cash flow is money you get from a real estate investment when the rental income you receive is more than the costs you incur, including maintenance, taxes, mortgage payments, and vacancy. When you buy a property right, finance it correctly, and control your expenses, you will achieve a positive net cash flow from the start. And, as rents increase over time, your cash flow can continue to grow.

Jim and Linda McKissack were already in their 40s and had four children when they began investing in real estate. Significance? They were looking for the fast-cash chance to rebuild their livelihood and eventually secure their financial future.

The couple came up with a plan to acquire 20 houses, financed on 15-year notes, and rent them at $1,000 a month. Since hitting this target, the McKissacks' plans, like most investors', have changed. With all properties performing, the couple's net worth has continued to grow, at the same time they keep collecting extra green each month. Over the years, they've leveraged the equity to acquire more properties—residential and commercial. Funny thing is, with so much financial security rolled up in their real estate portfolio today, they realized both stakes—cash flow and net worth—and retirement is something they no longer worry about.

Cash flow is king regardless of your personal criteria. If you make sure your property cash flows even $1/month from the get-go, you can hedge your bets on having made a good investment decision. But $1 is obviously not the end goal, so here are a few ways to achieve increased cash flow fast:

1. Put more cash down up front.

2. Amortize your mortgage on a 30-year note, for lower monthly payments.

3. Look at duplexes and small multifamily properties for multiple income streams.

4. Buy properties that are steeply discounted (foreclosures).

Increase Your Net Worth

Net worth, on the other hand, is the sum total of your assets and liabilities—what you own minus what you owe. It's the best and truest yardstick for calculating and keeping track of your financial success, and most wealthy people understand this. When you build your net worth, you increase your financial security over the long haul. With the HOLD strategy, you do this by paying down your mortgages and increasing your equity as quickly as possible. The question to ask here is: Where do you want to be in five years, in ten years, at age sixty-five? And, is building your net worth the best way to get there?

Steve Chader's son Matt bought his first investment property before he was twenty years old. With the luxury of time on his side, Matt pursued the HOLD strategy thinking in the long term. However, he still kept cash flow top of mind to guarantee each property a win. He did this by buying at the right price—meaning below market value—so that he made money going in. He financed his first property for thirty years to keep his monthly payments low, and he earned "sweat equity" by doing many home improvements himself. This not only allowed Matt to command higher rents, but ultimately to increase the value of his property—to add to his net worth.

Today, twenty years later, Matt has far exceeded his original net worth and cash flow goals and continues revisiting his plan to aim at hitting new targets. When it comes to upping your net worth, time is an amazing thing to have on your side. But, it's not the only way to increase your overall wealth using HOLD. You can also do the following:

1. Make sure to purchase on shorter amortization notes (e.g., a 15-year vs. a 30-year mortgage).

2. Be willing and able to make improvements to your HOLD properties for hidden added value, or buy "fixer-uppers" with the intent to add value.

3. Invest in single-family homes, which generally have higher appreciation rates than multifamily properties.

4. Accelerate your debt pay down—regardless of your mortgage length.

Stick to the Standards

The takeaway from both Matt and the McKissacks' stories is regardless of your original reason for investing—cash flow or net worth—there are always the bread-and-butter standards to help you make a wise investment in either capacity:

1. You *must not* violate cash flow. By this, we mean every property you invest in needs to cash flow at least $1 a month—we suggest closer to $100 a month—from the day you buy it.

2. Your net worth will increase on most any real estate investment through debt pay down, regardless of appreciation.

3. An ideal property might look something like this in year one—cash flows $150 to $200 per month; located in a decent enough neighborhood so that the property is not depreciating and has a reasonable expectation of average appreciation.

POINT TO REMEMBER

- Everyone brings their own story to the HOLD table. Likewise, every investor is in a unique place on her wealth-building journey. That's why it's important to remember to get as specific as possible on your mission and vision. The more focused your personal criteria are on the front end, the easier it will be to decipher your property criteria and achieve your wealth-building goals.

CHAPTER 2:
CREATE YOUR PROPERTY CRITERIA

1. FIND
The right property for the right terms and the right price

☑ **Chapter 1**: Create Your Personal Investment Criteria

☐ **Chapter 2**: Create Your Property Criteria

☐ **Chapter 3**: Lead Generate for Properties

Outcome: a list of qualified investment properties from which to choose

After reading this chapter, you will know how to:

☐ Define the investment neighborhoods to target.

☐ Determine the price and type of properties to target.

☐ Build the property criteria that's right for your HOLD investment strategy.

Now that you've established your personal investment criteria and determined *why* you buy, it's time to take the next step and pin down *where* and *what* you buy. With so many properties to choose from, how do you identify the best deals for you?

Your property investment criteria act as a litmus test against which you will weigh every property that comes your way; these standards remove the emotion from the process and ensure that each real estate transaction makes *good cents*! If the real estate "opportunity" involves numbers or factors that fall short of your criteria, you walk away and keep searching. It's that simple.

The price of the property is important, but it's only one of the factors to consider when establishing your investment criteria. The truth is not all houses are created equal. Some have a greater likelihood of appreciating more than others; some will produce greater cash flow. Others will be a maintenance nightmare and a drain on your profits.

Remember the tale of Goldilocks wandering into the home of the three bears? She tried out each chair, each bowl of porridge, and each bed until she found the one that was just right for her. By establishing your property investment criteria, doing your research, and sticking to your plan, you greatly increase your chances of finding the property that is just right for you.

THE RIGHT PROPERTY IN THE RIGHT PLACE

Not too long ago, an out-of-town investor came to Dallas, Texas, to buy an investment property. She had attended a seminar that touted the great deals to be had in the "Big D," and she was eager to stake her claim. Unfortunately, she ignored a cardinal rule: Know your market.

The investor didn't bother to research average rental rates in the area, nor did she research how the market differed from her own. Prices were so much lower in the Big D that she felt as if she were scooping up goodies from the bargain bin at a discount store. As you can imagine, the story did not have a happy ending—except for the seller and listing agent who sold her a property at retail price. The investor's willingness to skip due diligence led her to invest in properties that looked good on the surface but ended up costing her money in the end.

Moral of the story: It is not enough to hear that a particular area is "hot." As an investor, you need to be an expert or seek expert advice on your neighborhoods and the properties available in them. Property values can change from one block to the next and from builder to builder. Your goal as a new investor is to consciously start to make a habit of looking at your market and the properties available in it. Or again, rely on your agent or other investors. They are already able to recognize great opportunities and are there to help you spot deals.

Remember too that the goal of the HOLD strategy is to minimize your risk as much as possible while maximizing your returns. The so-called "hot" market—where prices can be inflated—might not represent the greatest long-term value for an investor.

There are five factors you should consider when you define your property criteria:

1. Location
2. Property Type
3. Economics
4. Condition
5. Features and Amenities

Let's consider these one at a time.

1. Location

The process of finding a great location is called "zeroing in" on your target market. In *FLIP: How to Find, Fix, and Sell Houses for Profit*, Rick Villani and Clay Davis shared a mapping exercise to zero in on neighborhoods that meet your target criteria. We are going to walk you through that exercise to help determine your hypothetical target neighborhoods in Springfield, a fictitious city in a nonspecified state.

First, find a map of your target city—similar to figure 2-1—that divides the region into neighborhoods, zip codes, or MLS-sectioned areas. Hint: Use the Internet so you don't have to zone the map yourself. If you can't find an image that works online, contact your real estate agent, who typically has access to presegmented area maps through the local Board of Realtors.

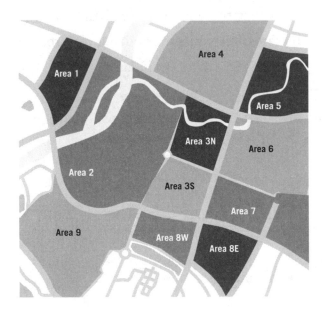

Figure 2-1

Second, using a pen or pencil, mark the areas where you live and work, and decide how far you're willing to travel to handle your investment properties. A 2012 survey of investors revealed that 79 percent purchase within thirty miles of home.* Keep in mind, you may be doing the maintenance and repairs on your first few properties, so having them in or near your neighborhood or where you work is not a bad option. Time is money, and you don't want to spend all your time on a commute.

Let's say you decide you are willing to drive a maximum of thirty minutes from home or work to get to your investment property. Since most of your property visits will take place outside of work hours, start by drawing a circle with a roughly thirty-mile circumference around your house. Then do the same around your office. Finally, connect the tops and bottoms of each circle—or look where they overlap—to highlight neighborhoods you already travel through on a daily basis.

Next, look for any and all areas that are not within your two circles or the path between them. Cross these out, as they do not fit your proximity criteria—see figure 2-2.

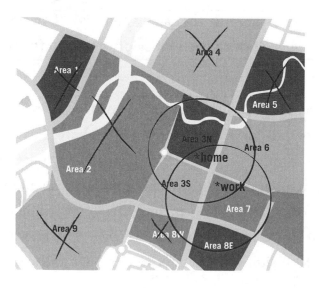

Figure 2-2

*2012 KW Market Navigator

Now look at each neighborhood within your prescribed boundaries. These neighborhoods will be your preliminary target areas—Area 3N, Area 3S, Area 6, Area 7, and Area 8E. You'll want to purposefully start spending time in each neighborhood within your circles—specifically the overlap—to get a better feel for the areas and collect more information on each. Remember Ms. Dallas' mistakes, and plan to devote some time to this part of the exercise. Tips to help you with this are:

- Talk to your agent, other local investors, and residents to get a firm grasp on the area (demographics, selling prices, average rents, historical property appreciation rates, rental vacancy ratios, and the percentage of rentals in the neighborhood).

- Plot new routes to and from work through a different neighborhood each week. Stop for coffee or meet a friend for dinner at local eateries, or do your weekly grocery shopping at a different supermarket. Being present in each neighborhood at various times throughout the day will help you grasp who lives there and what the scene in each area is like.

- Plan Sunday drives with the family and play "Eye Spy" looking for "For Sale" signs. Start to get an idea of what's on the market and for what price in each neighborhood.

- Ask questions. Don't be afraid to talk to locals. Some things you may want to know include: Do people want to live here? Is the neighborhood close to retail, office, and recreational areas? Are there nearby schools with good reputations? Is the neighborhood clean and well kept? Do the neighbors take pride in their homes? If a neighborhood mainly consists of single-family brick homes with 3 bedrooms and 2 baths, will a 2–1 with siding sell or rent for less? Do most of the houses in the neighborhood have garages or carports? What about washer-dryer connections? Are carpeting or wood floors standard? You'll need to understand the comparative pricing of properties in a target area to estimate the values of the houses there. This will also build your confidence when it's time to make an offer.

As you get more familiar with an area, jot down some neighborhood basics on your map. This may include the average list price for a single-family home and a duplex, neighborhood schools, the scene, and local activities/attractions. Look to figure 2-3 to see Springfield's varying MLS area characteristics.

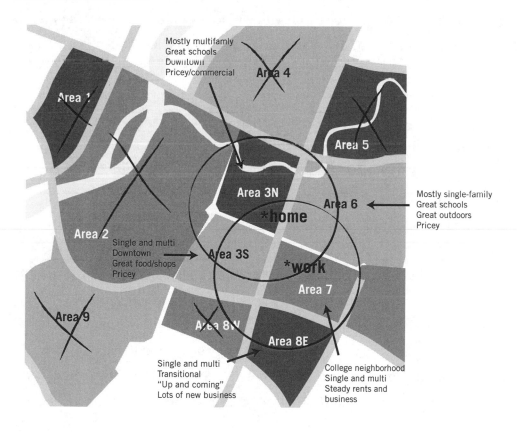

Figure 2-3

Once you've collected sufficient information on each prospective neighborhood, compare notes and look to your personal criteria to zero in on your final target areas. For instance, Area 6 is mostly single-family homes, so it's out since you want to keep your options open to small multifamily properties at this point. Similarly, Area 3N is comprised of mostly large multifamily and commercial spaces, so it's off the list as well. And Area 3S, though varying in property type, seems a bit pricey as it is in the heart of downtown. Let's cross it off too.

On the other hand, the two neighborhoods left on your map in figure 2-4—Area 7 and Area 8E—are what we will refer to as your target areas. These will be the locations you will focus on throughout the rest of your HOLD journey. Area 7 is a college neighborhood with both single and multifamily properties that seem to remain steady in pricing, rents, and business. They also have easy access to downtown and more outdoor activities. Area 8E, though a transitional neighborhood, offers both single and multifamily housing, and has had a rush of new businesses and families move in over the past two years, making it "up-and-coming." You may be able to find some good deals here.

Remember, you may have to revisit this exercise and your map as you continue to identify your property criteria in the rest of this section. And, as you become more familiar with the process and develop a reliable model, you may look for other areas to invest—perhaps a more outlying neighborhood or even another town. But proceed with caution. What looks like a good deal in one market may not be a good deal in another. At least in the beginning, it's much easier to stay on top of market changes, manage your portfolio, and monitor progress when the property is close at hand.

You're looking for desirable neighborhoods that maintain value and attract great tenants. That being said, it can be difficult for an investor to find opportunities in the most desirable neighborhoods. Because everyone wants to live there, prices tend to be higher. In that case, you should look on the fringes of the best areas or in transitional neighborhoods that are close to essential public services and systems but for various reasons are overlooked and undervalued.

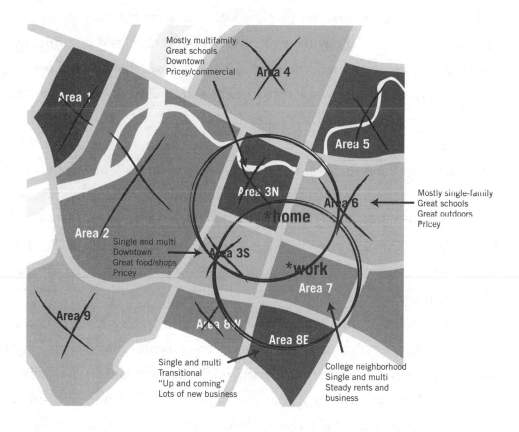

Figure 2-4

2. Property Type

The next question you should ask yourself is: single family or multifamily? Multifamily properties include duplexes, triplexes, fourplexes, and even larger condominium and apartment complexes. Most real estate investors will tell you that single-family homes offer the most reliable demand and appreciation, while multifamily properties offer cash flow. That's because single-family homes typically are bought by noninvestors who are willing to pay more for a home they like, while multifamily properties are bought and sold largely by investors. It's not a hard-and-fast rule, but investors who want to focus on building their net worth often will opt for single-family structures, while those interested in cash flow tend to seek multifamily structures for their portfolios.

Steve Chader, who began his investing career buying duplexes, sees advantages and disadvantages to buying multifamily properties. For example, if you own a fourplex and one unit goes vacant, you still have three units bringing in rent. On the other hand, with multifamily, you have more tenants and possibly more maintenance and oversight. Because of this, most investors tend to demand higher ROI from multifamily than single-family properties.

Some areas of the country no longer zone parcels for two-, three-, and fourplexes, which means that many of the neighborhoods with a high concentration of multifamily properties might be older and on the decline. However, there are still areas that have a mix of multifamily and single-family homes in good neighborhoods with good schools and amenities nearby, which make them great places to invest. In fact, some investors target duplexes in these mixed neighborhoods, where they can purchase based on cash flow, and still have the option of selling the property retail to a homeowner who wants to live on one side.

The question of whether to focus on single family or multifamily depends on what you want: the appreciation and relative stability of a single-family home, or multiple streams of income that help build your cash flow. For example's sake, we are going to focus on areas of Springfield that offer both to show you varying outcomes as we work through the HOLD strategy. Make sure to eliminate any target markets that don't meet your property type criteria.

3. Economics

Any seasoned investor will tell you that you don't know what a property is really worth until you've built your economic criteria, which include price, discount rate, projected cash flow, and appreciation.

The biggest reason investors don't make money is simple: They pay too much for a property. Your profit should be locked in immediately once you buy the property—make your money going in. How? Buy below fair market value. But first, you need to know what you can afford to make sure your target neighborhoods' values are not above your means. To do this, make an appointment with your lender to decipher your prequalification price.

As mentioned in the overview, your agent should be able to recommend a lender for you to work with. Schedule an initial meeting to review your current investments and assets. You will be asked to fill out a form with information such as your current bank account stats, monthly rent or mortgage payments, employer, salary, list of other investments, list of credit cards, etc. After running your paperwork through her system, your lender will be able to tell you a price you are prequalified for based on varying down payment amounts. We suggest getting both single-family and duplex prequalification numbers, as the increased rental income on a multifamily will typically up the price point you can afford.

Your prequalification number is a great jumping off price point. However, be sure to follow up with the appropriate documentation to your lender for preapproval. You cannot move forward on a property without preapproval.

Let's say you have been preapproved for a $170,000 single-family home and a $250,000 duplex. Revisit your map of Springfield neighborhoods, figure 2-4 on p. 19, and cross off any areas that, on average, exceed this price point. Again, your agent will be able to get you the common fair market value of each neighborhood in your target regions. Luckily, Area 7 and Area 8E are both within range, so we'll just add the fair market value prices to our map in figure 2-5.

Once you've done this, you can start using your price range to compare properties in your target neighborhoods. Getting a better idea of what your money can typically buy you will help you notice deals when they come on the market. We suggest trying to find a discount rate of at least 10 percent. That's built-in equity—you make your money going in. In areas with high average price points, 10 percent is a bit unrealistic. For these areas, we suggest picking a target discount amount (say $15,000) and sticking to that as your guide.

Another very important economic criterion is cash flow. Remember, cash flow is king, and bread-and-butter properties will cash flow $100–$200 monthly from the start. Aside from asking neighbors and

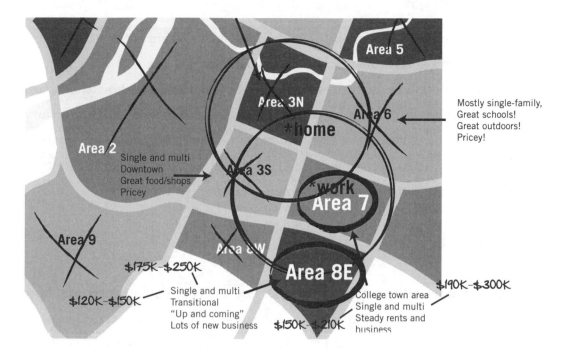

Figure 2-5

other investors in the area for average rent prices, we will help you pull comparables and drive the numbers in "Analyze" to make sure your property will produce. Unfortunately, we've seen many people lose investment properties due to negative cash flow. In most instances, these folks were betting their properties would appreciate enough to justify their investment. It's important to realize that playing the appreciation game is for speculators, not investors.

As we mentioned earlier, though the median appreciation rate over the last thirty years is 4.4 percent, this number varies depending on time, neighborhood, and even street block. So, even though you are not going to rely on appreciation, it is worth investigating what rates have been in your target areas. Every neighborhood should have a historical track record when it comes to value and appreciation. Your real estate agent can help you determine the best potential appreciation rate for a specific neighborhood. The historical track record will show you how the actual market views the values in that area rather than somebody's arbitrary projection of what appreciation to expect. But remember, appreciation happens in the future and you can't control it, so don't make it the basis of your criteria. It's your added bonus, your icing on the cake.

4. Condition

The condition of a property is another key driver of your criteria, and how much cash you have may dictate this for you. While properties in poor condition often sell at discounted prices, their repair costs can tap your cash reserves on the back end.

A house in visible disrepair may indicate that the owner is short of money and needs to sell quickly or that it's rented to a tenant who isn't maintaining the property. Either way, it may present an opportunity for profit, especially if you're a do-it-yourself person who wants to handle the repairs, or you already have cash and a team of contractors at the ready. The more work a property requires, the greater the discount should be. Beginning investors with little construction experience would be better advised to start with properties that need only minor repairs. But, for those of you more experienced or handy investors, don't forget the option to flip. *FLIP: How to Find, Fix, and Sell Houses for Profit*, *HOLD*'s companion book in the Millionaire Real Estate Investor series, is a good place to start when contemplating this related journey.

The age of a property can also be a positive or a negative, depending on its location. Typically, the older a house is, the more maintenance it will require and the less it will appeal to prospective tenants. However, there are desirable neighborhoods where older houses are thought to have more character. Something else to consider: An older house may have been owned by the same person for a longer period of time, meaning the owner has more equity in the house and might be willing to accept a lower offer. And, the maintenance risk can often be mitigated by purchasing a home warranty. Keep this in mind as you look at properties on a case-by-case basis.

5. Features and Amenities

The features of a property are its basic descriptive elements—number of bedrooms, number of bathrooms, number of stories, and whether the home has a garage, carport, or neither. The features you include in your criteria will depend on the neighborhoods you target. If all the properties in your target area have 3 bedrooms, 3 baths, and a 2-car garage, then that's what you should seek. Anything less will have an adverse effect on the property value and rental rates. Get a feel for the "neighborhood norm." A home that conforms to the neighborhood norm is typically a safer bet.

Amenities are the extras, such as energy-efficient improvements or "built-ins," custom cabinetry, or exterior improvements, such as an outdoor living area or swimming pool. They may not be something you include in your criteria, but they should be noted. Some amenities for homeowners—such as a pool—can actually be a liability for investors because of maintenance and insurance costs. On the other hand, amenities can make an average property have greater value or offset any deficiencies—for instance, a 2-bed, 1-bath home in a neighborhood where most homes have two or more bathrooms. Amenities can also allow you to command a higher monthly rent. A property manager can help you determine how much additional rent you can or cannot charge based on your amenities.

Let's say your target neighborhoods in Springfield offer, on average at your price point, 3–2 single families, with a carport, built in the 1960s to 2000s, on less than a quarter acre of land. Pools are a toss-up, but for investment purposes you are looking for properties without pools. Similarly, Springfield duplexes are a bit pricier for 2–2/2–1 units, with garages, built in the 1960s to 1980s, on less than a quarter acre of land, often with a community recreation center and pool.

Now it's time to learn price points from experts who are familiar with your neighborhoods. Why reinvent the wheel? Many investors have come before you. Use their knowledge and mistakes on your journey to wealth. Keep in mind, it is important to know what the missions are for the investors you take advice from. If their requirements are different than yours, their advice should be taken with a grain of salt.

ASK THE EXPERTS

Once you've established criteria for location, property type, economics, condition, and features and amenities, revisit your zeroing in map. Make sure you have x-ed out all neighborhoods that do not fit your personal or property criteria. For instance, you should have narrowed Springfield to two target areas, Area 7 and Area 8E, as seen previously in figure 2-5.

Once you're confident about your target neighborhoods, do some research to get the names of property managers and other real estate agents and investors who are familiar with the areas. Call them and tell them that you're an investor looking to purchase property. Then ask them questions. Most will be willing to answer you because you could be a source for future business. Some questions to ask might include:

- What price range of rental properties is in highest demand among renters?

- What price range is the most difficult to rent?

- What areas in the neighborhood have the highest rental demand and why? Is it the school district, proximity to shopping, business and recreation centers, or the overall amenities?

- Is there a local rule of thumb or standard for determining the rental rate? For instance, if a home is valued at $100,000, what will the rent likely be? What about for a duplex?

- If applicable, what online tools do you use to determine rents in your area or city?

- What features cause the home to rent more quickly and the tenants to pay higher prices?

- Is there anything I should have asked that I didn't?

Take plenty of notes during your interview. You'll be getting valuable information that will help you continue to build your criteria and improve your decision making.

The HOLD Investor's Criteria Worksheet

1. LOCATION

State/Province

- [ ] Taxes
- [ ] Rental Laws
- [ ] Weather

Street

- [ ] Traffic
- [ ] Size

County/Parish _____

City/Town

- [ ] Taxes
- [ ] Services
- [ ] Neighborhood
- [ ] School District
- [ ] Crime
- [ ] Transportation
- [ ] Shopping/Rec

Lot

- [ ] Zoning
- [ ] Adjoining Lots
- [ ] Lot Size
- [ ] Trees
- [ ] Privacy
- [ ] Landscaping
- [ ] View

2. PROPERTY TYPE

Single Family

- [ ] Home
- [ ] Condo
- [ ] Townhome
- [ ] Mobile Home
- [ ] Zero Lot

- [ ] Duplex
- [ ] Fourplex
- [ ] Large Multi/Commercial
- [ ] Land/Lot
- [ ] New/Preconstruction
- [ ] Resale

- [ ] Urban
- [ ] Suburban
- [ ] Exurban
- [ ] Rural
- [ ] Resort/Vacation
- [ ] Farm/Ranch

3. ECONOMICS

- [ ] From $_____ to $_____
- [ ] Discount _____%

- [ ] Cash Flow $_____/Mo.
- [ ] Appreciation _____%/Yr.

4. CONDITION AND CONSTRUCTION

- [ ] Needs No Repair
- [ ] Needs Minor Cosmetic
- [ ] Needs Major Cosmetic
- [ ] Needs Structural
- [ ] Needs Demolition

- [ ] Roof
- [ ] Walls
- [ ] Foundation
- [ ] Plumbing
- [ ] Water/Waste

- [ ] Wiring
- [ ] Insulation
- [ ] Heating/AC
- [ ] _____
- [ ] _____

5. FEATURES AND AMENITIES

- [ ] Age/Year Built _____
- [ ] Beds _____
- [ ] Baths _____
- [ ] Living _____
- [ ] Dining _____

- [ ] Stories _____
- [ ] Size _____ Sq. Ft.
- [ ] Ceilings _____ Ft.
- [ ] Parking/Garage
- [ ] Kitchen

- [ ] Closets/Storage
- [ ] Appliances (Gas/Electric)
- [ ] Floor Plan
- [ ] _____
- [ ] _____

PUT IT ALL TOGETHER

After zeroing in, take a minute and make sure your criteria are in place before you do anything else. Figure 2-6 provides a concise checklist of possible "wants" and "needs" to keep top of mind for each category.

As you look over this worksheet, keep in mind that, yes, as you become a more experienced investor, your criteria may change. And yes, when you become an expert, you may base criteria on rules of thumb—cap rates, gross rent multipliers, rent-to-value ratios—but remember, you must earn that right. Until then, due diligence and hard math is the way to enter an investment.

And your agent can help. By providing him with three main criteria from your exercise—location, price, and property type—he can help set you up with online searches and property listings that fit your initial bill. This will provide you with a steady stream of properties for sale in your target market to look at and compare.

HOLDing Takes Time and Trial

Look at the McKissacks. Only after much trial and error did Jim and Linda develop super fine-tuned criteria that worked for them, in their market, and for their investment strategy.

When they started out, they looked for older houses because they loved the character and charm. They still own several of these, which remain great investments. But, generally speaking, older homes are no longer in their criteria after years of dealing with mold issues, roof leaks, foundation problems, and repairs that reduce cash flow.

Jim and Linda's investment criteria today consist of 3- and 4-bedroom brick homes, ten years old or less, in established neighborhoods, not more than thirty minutes from where they live. The home also must demand the maximum rent for that area, with average rates of appreciation for the market. If the McKissacks can purchase it below market value, then it looks like they found a winner.

Greg Sofio, an investor in New Mexico, also has very specific criteria. "When I first started holding properties twenty-five years ago, I was in my early 20s and had no sophistication. I trusted my gut," he admits.

Early in his investing career, Greg looked for single-family homes in the path of commercial development. He would hold them until developers came along with an offer because they wanted to make room for a gas station or strip center.

"Today I look for single-family properties that are 4-bedroom, 2-bath, with a 2-car garage, less than ten years old, in blue-collar, working-class neighborhoods," he says. "I can rent out those kinds of houses all day long. A $500,000 or $600,000 house may be nicer, but that isn't a payment I want to make if it's vacant.

"If a house that rents for $1,000 per month is vacant for a month, that's the cost of doing business," Greg continues, adding that if the house costs you $3,500 to $4,000 a month, it's not the wisest investment.

POINTS TO REMEMBER

It's easy to "trust your gut," but it's not the way smart investors make money in real estate. Rely on your instincts, but only after you have the knowledge and criteria in place to inform them. Keep these five factors top of mind when narrowing the criteria for your target property:

- Location

- Property Type

- Economics

- Condition

- Features and Amenities

Combined with expert advice, this will put you in a great place to start narrowing your vision and finding prospects.

CHAPTER 3:
LEAD GENERATE FOR PROPERTIES

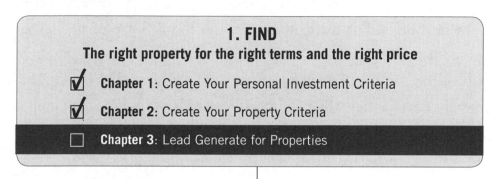

Outcome: a list of qualified investment properties from which to choose

After reading this chapter, you will know how to:

☐ Cultivate and deploy a network to support your search.

☐ Prospect target areas for investment opportunities.

☐ Market for opportunities.

USE YOUR INVESTOR'S EYE

As an investor, you're not looking for just any house. There's a difference between the retail market, which is where the typical home buyer shops, and the wholesale market, where real estate investors buy. Retail buyers want to buy value too. They want the best house in the best condition for the best price. But their primary motivation is not profit. They are moving for personal reasons—a spouse, a new job, a baby, a new school, etc. Investors, on the other hand, are primarily motivated by profit. They have tight criteria they won't violate. If a retail buyer is willing to look at eight to twelve properties to find a home, an investor might look at 100 to identify one with real investment potential.

While retail buyers typically pass on houses that are vacant or in disrepair, investors love ugly ducklings. They understand cosmetic flaws can be fixed, and money is made fixing problems others are unwilling to deal with. Investors investigate every lead or leverage in the negotiation.

Your goal is to find a house that meets your criteria: the right house in the right place at the right price. Because you have specific criteria and are willing to cast a wide net, you will need a large volume of leads to generate enough opportunities that will result in a successful purchase. Leads—information that "leads" you to a potential property—are the foundation of your HOLD journey.

LEAD GENERATE

There are basically three ways to lead generate for investment properties. You can network, prospect, or market. Networking is simply leveraging relationships to find potential properties through the people that own them. Prospecting is when you hit the streets and devote direct time and energy to finding opportunities. And, if prospecting is something you do, marketing is something you unleash. Through signs, mailers, ads, and fliers, you're spreading your message to a broad audience.

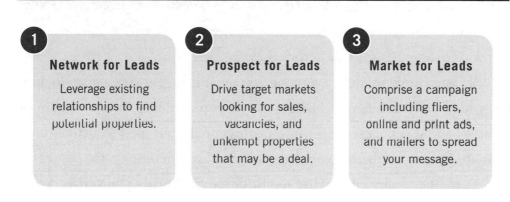

HOLD's Three Lead-Generating Methods

1
Network for Leads
Leverage existing relationships to find potential properties.

2
Prospect for Leads
Drive target markets looking for sales, vacancies, and unkempt properties that may be a deal.

3
Market for Leads
Comprise a campaign including fliers, online and print ads, and mailers to spread your message.

Figure 3-1

You can use one or any combination of the methods discussed in this chapter. How much time you have to generate leads will determine which strategies you deploy. Choose what fits best with your current routine and lifestyle.

1. Network for Leads

Networking provides two things: knowledge and leads. A wise investor will seek the advice and experience of others. There are many people who have walked the investment path before, and it's to your advantage to learn from their mistakes instead of repeating them. Also, sharing your criteria with a wide-ranging network greatly increases the number of promising leads sent your way.

Your network should include both property owners and local experts—real estate agents who work in your target areas, real estate lawyers and accountants, courthouse clerks, and title company professionals. These people are in an excellent position to pass leads to you. Also, every banker in town needs to know that you buy investment property. If anyone knows about the local real estate market, it's a banker. Bankers may know of properties for sale before they are listed.

If you think about it, everyone you meet can generate a lead, including your family, friends, and neighbors. If you regularly hire lawn-care or housekeeping services, even these professionals can alert you to homes that are getting ready to go on the market or are opening up for new renters. You'll be surprised at what might come of sharing your criteria and plans with others, and you should do it often.

And, if you're looking for new networking opportunities, two groups definitely stand out when looking for investment property: real estate agents and investment clubs.

Network	
☐ Seminars	☐ Neighborhood Associations
☐ Friends and Family	☐ Courthouse Proceedings
☐ Business Colleagues	☑ Real Estate Agents
☐ Community Events	☑ REI Clubs
☐ Lenders	☐ Attorneys

Figure 3-2

Real estate agents

For investors who simply don't have the time to generate leads or who want more leads than they can produce on their own, real estate agents can provide a pipeline of opportunities. The good ones know their markets inside-and-out and often hear about great deals before they hit the market. They can give you full access to information on the MLS, which includes average home values and rents in the area. Get referrals to agents who understand investing and work with investors. Be aware, however, that if you use the "neighborhood specialist" real estate agent, he or she has a reputation to protect in the neighborhood and will likely be working to get the highest price.

Real estate investment clubs

Real estate investment clubs, which have been springing up in many cities, are great places to expand your network. You'll meet other real estate investors—from novice to seasoned—as well as lenders, builders, tradespeople, and vendors. At club meetings, you can share war stories and get recommendations on property managers, mortgage companies, and building contractors. These are people who have direct access to sellers and houses you're seeking.

Over the years, the McKissacks have used their network to grow their capabilities and skills. Linda's advice is to seek out the "knowledge leaders" in your area and ask for fifteen minutes of their time. Prepare a list of questions, including how they got started in investing and what they have learned. Find out who they know and ask them to refer you. You'll be surprised after only three or four of these interviews how much valuable knowledge and insight you will gain.

Don't forget: Your network is a two-way street. These relationships aren't solely about what others can do for you. Help the people who are helping you by passing along business leads, offering finder's fees, or proposing a share of the business venture.

Be courteous in all your business dealings. Send thank-you notes, and honor your commitments. Keep your promises and do what you say you will do. You're not just building relationships—you're building your reputation, which is what gives people the confidence to do business with you. All business plans, innovative ideas, and strategies are meaningless without it.

2. Prospect for Leads

As you know, prospecting is an act that takes time and energy. But skilled investors know there are simple ways to build prospecting into your weekly and even daily life, regardless of your schedule. You see, prospecting is really just constantly keeping an eye out and an ear open.

There are four types of properties you prospect for: listings, vacancies, for sale by owner (FSBO) properties, and pre-foreclosures or foreclosures. Each can be found by building new routines into your preexisting everyday habits.

Prospect
I. Listings
II. Vacancies
III. For Sale by Owner (FSBO) Properties
IV. Pre-foreclosures or Foreclosures

Figure 3-3

Everyone gathers news on a daily basis in one way or another. Whether you enjoy the morning paper each day with a cup of coffee, spend time surfing the Web on your lunch break, or watch the ten o'clock news after everyone is tucked in bed, staying abreast of local and worldwide happenings is something that's safe to say everyone makes time for. So, why not use this habit as a prompt to look for listings?

Yes, most newspapers still have a real estate section—after you're done with the sports page, flip back and scan the market's latest additions. And these days, the Internet has made online listing searches quite simple, but since you've already established a relationship with your real estate agent, why not tap their resources as well? Most agents are not only willing and able to prospect for you and send matching listings your way, they can actually set you up on one or many "portal or drip campaigns" to receive MLS listings matching your criteria on a daily basis. Of course, there's always the daily commute or shuttle bus to various after-school activities. Make a family game out of hunting down for-sale signs, and take note of properties that look appealing. A visit to the nearby courthouse could also help buy some time and provide information on current pre-foreclosures or foreclosures. Who knows, you may even stumble upon an auction while your son is at his guitar lesson.

However, some of the best investment opportunities can be found when you take a perceived "burden" off someone else's hands and turn it into a cash-flowing commodity. These gems are typically not listed on the MLS, but rather are found in similar fashion to a scavenger hunt.

An empty house represents money that someone is losing. Fortunately for you, investors know how to spot such opportunities. And, similar to listings, the habits you need for prospecting vacant houses are synonymous with your preexisting, everyday actions—your commute, driving kids to school and practice, early-morning or after-dinner walks, etc.

As you explore your target neighborhoods, look for properties with advertising circulars piling up on the front lawn, overflowing mailboxes, missing shingles, faded or peeling exterior paint, and a general air of disrepair. These are usually all signs that no one lives there, or that the owner doesn't have the money to make the needed repairs. Either way, it could spell opportunity for the savvy investor.

Talk to the neighbors. They may be able to tell you the owner's name and his or her situation. They'll probably be happy to help if they think you might relieve them of the neighborhood eyesore. To glean more information, you can search online by the owner's name or the physical address, or visit the tax assessor's office. In this market, the owner may be a bank who hasn't put the home up for sale yet.

You probably won't be able to get the telephone number, but try calling directory assistance or using Internet directories to get the number. Some counties post ownership information on their websites. Once you have the phone number, call the owner and offer to buy the property or ask whether he or she might consider selling. At the very least, ask the owner to keep in touch.

Many out-of-town owners may not be aware of the condition of their properties and may be motivated to sell if you send them current photos of their homes. Even if they don't want to sell, you could be the first person they call when they change their minds.

III. For sale by owner (FSBO) properties

There are many reasons owners try to sell a property without using a real estate agent. Maybe they're trying to avoid agent fees, or maybe they think they don't have enough equity in the home to afford a traditional sale. Whatever the reason, FSBOs present a great opportunity for investors. Without a real estate agent to drive prospective buyers, these properties can end up sitting on the market longer. And time on the market can amp up the owner's willingness to sell.

The owner may be willing to sell the home at a discount or make some other arrangement, such as owner financing or allowing you to assume the mortgage. Because these owners think they are saving money by not paying a listing agent a commission, you could make an offer that equates to the asking price minus the commission and still arrive at an acceptable price for both parties. But, unless you are a real estate agent, you'd be wise to leave room for the buyer agent's compensation so you can be properly represented in the transaction.

Again, newspapers are a great place to find FSBOs. Phrases like "motivated seller" or "handyman special" may tip off a possible good deal. Other places to look are lead generation sites that list properties "for sale by owner." Or you can simply drive around your target neighborhood and look for FSBO signs.

One last word on FSBOs: Owners tend to overprice their properties, so you'll need to be knowledgeable about property values in the neighborhood when you approach the seller. Ask your agent to pull some recent sales comps for you.

IV. Pre-foreclosures or foreclosures

Buying property "on the courthouse steps"—where foreclosures are auctioned once a month, once a week, or even daily—isn't for the faint of heart or novice investors. Before you attend an auction, you need to educate yourself on how auctions are conducted, what special ground rules apply in your state, and what risks are involved. Attend several auctions to observe the process. You'll learn a lot just by observing and listening.

You also should be prepared to do plenty of research ahead of time to determine if the property is encumbered with unpaid property taxes, tax liens, or other outstanding judgments. Properties due to be foreclosed are listed publicly in advance of the proceedings. After combing the list for properties that match your criteria, you should proceed straight to Stage 2: Analyze to work out an appropriate offer. Unlike a traditional sale, all your research needs to be complete *before* you make your offer. There will be no closing to negotiate later.

Many professional investors have made a killing buying pre-foreclosures and foreclosures at bargain rates. But if you're not willing to do the necessary legwork, you may be the one getting "killed."

3. Market for Leads

If you've ever noticed a billboard or yard sign that states: "We pay cash for houses," or "Need fast cash for your house?" you're witnessing a real estate investor's lead generation strategy in action. Advertising is a great way to get the word out and attract sellers. Even something as simple as an ongoing newspaper ad with the words, "We buy houses for cash," will attract a supply of potential sellers in need of fast cash.

Direct-mail advertising—postcards, fliers, or other items with your name and sales message on them—is a tried-and-true technique to help establish you as the investor/buyer in your target neighborhood. Even a business card tacked on the bulletin board at the local grocery store will let people know that you're the person to call if they want to sell their homes.

As you grow your business, you may want to invest in radio or TV advertising to extend your reach and maximize your advertising dollars. Keep track of which ads generate the most responses and continue to refine your game plan. Consistent advertising has a cumulative effect: the more you keep your name in front of potential sellers, the more likely they are to think of you when they are ready to sell. Your real estate agent can be a great partner in this effort.

Market for Leads

I.   Create billboards or yard signs – "We pay cash for houses!"
II. Send direct mailings including your name and sales message.
III. Invest in radio or TV ads to extend your reach.
IV. Include ad dollars in your price of purchase.

Figure 3-4

Finding seller leads through advertising is where you set in motion your marketing strategy and let it work for you. People will always have circumstances in their lives that cause them to sell their properties. Let them know they have a willing, reliable buyer who is able to act quickly.

When potential sellers call, be honest with them. Let them know that you're an investor who doesn't plan to live in the property. Also, emphasize that the property must meet your criteria and terms. After you've completed your analysis, you can offer to buy the property at a predetermined price if they aren't able to sell it at a retail price in a certain number of days.

It's true that many of the people who will contact you will be in desperate situations—facing foreclosures, crushing debts, or divorces. It may seem as though you are profiting on someone else's misfortune, but if you are honest and fair in your dealings, you are providing a reasonable option that otherwise wouldn't have been presented.

When your advertising pays off with responses, conduct some due diligence to weed out false leads and identify the sellers you want to meet. Some questions you'll want to ask are:

- Are you the owner? If not, what is the owner's number so I can contact him/her?

- Where is the house? (You only want to pursue properties in your target neighborhoods.)

- What kind of house is it? (Number of bedrooms, size of lot, is it brick or wood construction?)

- How old is the house and are repairs needed?

- Why are you selling?

- Are your payments current, or are back payments, taxes, or homeowners association dues owed?

- How soon do you need to move?

- What do you hope to accomplish by selling this property?

- What is your selling price and what kind of financial arrangements do you propose?

- Would you consider offering terms?

- If you don't sell, what will you do?

Let's say you've now told all of your friends, family, and colleagues that you're looking to invest in a 3–2 single-family home under $200,000 in Area 7 or Area 8E, or a duplex under $300,000 in the same neighborhood. You've also made it a habit to venture through your two target Springfield investment areas on your daily bike ride and spend twenty minutes at night sifting through your MLS notices. Say after a few months of searching, you find two properties—one single-family, one duplex—on the same street in Area 7.

742 Evergreen Terrace	127 Elm Street
Single-family home	Multifamily duplex
3–2 floor plan with garage	2–2 and 2–1 floor plan with carport
1,200 sq. ft.	850 sq. ft. and 750 sq. ft.
Year built: 1984	Year built: 1979
List price: $150,000	List price: $210,000
Currently unoccupied	Currently rented
No rental history	Units rent for: $1,125 and $850/month
Details: cement foundation, all-brick exterior, carpet and vinyl flooring	Details: cement foundation, all-brick exterior, carpet and vinyl flooring

Will either of these properties make a wise HOLD investment? In "Analyze," the next stage in the HOLD model, you'll learn how to review a list of promising prospects and identify the property that is most worthy of your investment dollars through a side-by-side comparison of the two Springfield finds. We will continue using these "target" properties throughout this book to walk you through the entire HOLD process.

POINTS TO REMEMBER

There are three ways to keep your finger on the pulse of properties that meet your criteria:

- Networking

- Prospecting

- Marketing

And, once you find the one lead-generating strategy that works best for you, you'll be surprised how many investment opportunities arise.

STAGE 2: ANALYZE

✓

1. FIND
The right property for the right terms and the right price

Outcome: a list of qualified investment properties from which to choose

2. ANALYZE
A property to make sure the numbers and the terms make sense

- ☐ **Chapter 4**: Understand Your HOLD Worksheet
- ☐ **Chapter 5**: Estimate the Purchase Price
- ☐ **Chapter 6**: Project the Rent
- ☐ **Chapter 7**: Calculate the Costs
- ☐ **Chapter 8**: Analyze the Property

Outcome: a prospect that meets your financial criteria

Life is like a combination lock: your job is to find the right numbers,
in the right order, so you can have anything you want.

Brian Tracy

"Analyze" is when it starts to get real. Through the Find process, you narrowed a long list of properties that looked promising to a few that meet your personal and property criteria. Now comes that moment of truth when you put your prospects under the magnifying glass. This is the part where you assume the mantle of the dispassionate detective. A potential opportunity only becomes credible when there is evidence to support it!

"Analyze" is the most important step in the HOLD journey. It serves two purposes: It provides a deliberate process for clear-eyed, good decisions, and it helps you avoid reckless ones. The biggest mistake people make when buying an investment property is to let emotion cloud their judgment. They buy a property even when the numbers don't make sense. They've read the books, attended the seminars, and even announced to their friends and family that they're making the leap into real estate investing. It's an exciting time. Then, after weeks spent browsing Internet listings, combing neighborhoods, and visiting properties with their agent, they finally have a potential investment property, and their emotions get stirred up.

Honor your fear. Listen to it and then answer. The only way to make it go away is due diligence—you have to run the numbers. And, if the numbers work, your fears will be silenced. Ignore your impatience. Yes, another investor may well "steal" your find. Experienced investors can analyze properties much faster than novices...it's a fact. They've had more practice, and that's okay—they can have it. You'll find another one. You have to adopt an attitude of abundance.

It is far better to miss ten great investment properties than it is to buy one bad one. The financial stakes are high and should be taken seriously. You don't want to start by digging a financial hole. Each great investment you make will add to your confidence and create financial momentum for your life.

As much as "Analyze" should be about the cold, hard facts, the reality is that emotions are bound to arise. Deal with them honestly and head-on. Follow the numbers and try to have fun.

The financial analysis of an investment property may seem daunting, but with the tools and information provided here, you'll have a straightforward process to decide which properties to buy and which to walk away from.

Some investors use elaborate spreadsheet calculations, while some are more "back of the envelope" types. We've split the difference and created an easy-to-use worksheet—available for download on the HOLD page at www.KellerINK.com—around some of the key numbers investors focus on when analyzing properties: purchase price, rental income, expenses, mortgage payment, net income, and cash flow. Due to the detailed, long-term math generated by the HOLD Property Analysis Worksheet available for download on www.KellerINK.com, some of the numbers in our hypothetical analysis will have been rounded.

So even if you have to spend a little extra time and effort here, it may be the best investment you ever make in yourself. Analysis is the heart of investing, and our HOLD Property Analysis Worksheet will help you the whole way through.

CHAPTER 4:
UNDERSTAND YOUR HOLD WORKSHEET

✓
1. FIND
The right property for the right terms and the right price

Outcome: a list of qualified investment properties from which to choose

2. ANALYZE
A property to make sure the numbers and the terms make sense

☐ **Chapter 4**: Understand Your HOLD Worksheet

☐ **Chapter 5**: Estimate the Purchase Price

☐ **Chapter 6**: Project the Rent

☐ **Chapter 7**: Calculate the Costs

☐ **Chapter 8**: Analyze the Property

Outcome: a prospect that meets your financial criteria

After reading this chapter, you will know how to:

☐ Size up your prospects.

☐ Use your HOLD Property Analysis Worksheet.

BUILD YOUR HOLD PROPERTY ANALYSIS WORKSHEET

The HOLD Property Analysis Worksheet outlines the numbers that smart investors take into account when sizing up leads. (Again, this worksheet is available for download on the HOLD page at www.KellerINK.com.) In the following chapters, you'll learn how to use your worksheet, and how each line item impacts your bottom line. For the teaching purposes of this book, we will use the HOLD worksheet to analyze the two Springfield properties you found in "Find"—a single-family home and a duplex.

Let's take a closer look at those two properties mentioned at the end of chapter 3. If you recall, 742 Evergreen Terrace is a single-family home in Area 7 of Springfield. It's listed for $150,000 with no current rental history. On the other hand, 127 Elm Street is a duplex in the same neighborhood listed for $210,000 with both units currently rented—one for $1,125/month, and one for $850/month. Both properties are brick structures built on cement foundations with a carpet/vinyl mix for flooring and need some cosmetic improvements, but appear to be structurally sound.

Running the numbers on the two prospects will allow you to arrive at a maximum offer price that makes each a great investment. But what are the numbers you need to know to properly analyze and decide which property to buy? How do you research them? And when can you feel confident that you have a clear picture of the property's investment potential? To answer these questions, we're going to look at and fill out the HOLD Property Analysis Worksheet section by section until you have a working document to guide you to your best HOLD opportunity.

Two Springfield Prospects

742 Evergreen Terrace

Single-family home

3–2 floor plan with garage

1,200 sq. ft.

Year built: 1984

List price: $150,000

Currently unoccupied; no rental history

Details: cement foundation, all brick exterior, carpet and vinyl flooring

127 Elm Street

Multifamily duplex

2–2 and 2–1 floor plan with carport

890 sq. ft. and 750 sq. ft.

Year built: 1979

List price: $210,000

Rents for: $1,125 and $850

Currently rented

Details: cement foundation, all brick exterior, carpet and vinyl flooring

Figure 4-1

In figure 4-2 on p. 54, you see a blank HOLD Property Analysis Worksheet. Some of the blanks are easy to fill in—for instance, add your name and your agent's name in the spaces labeled "Prepared By" and "Client Name." Then fill in the property address.

For the purpose of this exercise, we'll use assumptions based on long-term historical averages for some of the numbers, specifically mortgage interest rates, home price and rent appreciation rates, as well as cost of sale. Mortgage interest rates tend to be similar across markets but they are very timely, changing from week to week and month to month. While we're using a 30-year median, it's highly likely you can get far better rates in recent years. Home price and rent appreciation rates are based on 20-year national averages. Depending on your local market, these may seem high or low. Finally, our cost of sale is based on the historic average cost to sell a home at 7 percent. This is based on the assumption that you will list with a real estate agent, your buyer will be similarly represented, and that

HOLD Property Analysis Worksheet

Prepared By _____   Client Name _____

Property Address _____   List Price _____

I. Fair Market Value

Discount (%,$)	_____ %	$_____
Purchase Price (max offer price)	$_____	
Percent Down	_____ %	
Down Payment Amount	$_____	
Amount Financed	$_____	
Interest Rate	_____ %	
Costs of Repairs (make-ready)	$_____	
Length of Mortgage (years)	_____	

	Monthly	Annual
Mortgage Payment	$_____	$_____

II. Rental Income

	Monthly	Annual
Unit A	$_____	$_____
Unit B	$_____	$_____
Unit C	$_____	$_____
Unit D	$_____	$_____
Gross Rental Income	$_____	$_____
Vacancy Rate	_____ %	_____ %
Net Rental Income	$_____	$_____

III. Expenses

	Monthly	Annual
Property Management Fees	$_____	$_____
Leasing Costs	$_____	$_____
Maintenance Reserve	$_____	$_____
Utilities	$_____	$_____
Property Taxes	$_____	$_____
Insurance	$_____	$_____
Other (HOA fees, lawn care, trash, etc.)	$_____	$_____
Total Expenses	$_____	$_____

IV. Net Operating Income

	Monthly	Annual
	$_____	$_____
Mortgage Payment	$_____	$_____
Net Cash Flow	$_____	$_____

Investment Analysis

Total Cash In (down payment + repairs)	$_____
Appreciation Rate (20 yr. avg. = 4.4%)	4.4%
Rent Appreciation (20 yr. avg. = 3.1%)	3.1%

Figure 4-2

you'll have some ancillary closing costs. Please note, while all these numbers are conservative and reasonable for the purposes of this *hypothetical* analysis, in a *real* investment analysis, you will always use current and local information. Always leverage the professionals on your HOLD team for accurate, timely, and local information!

The four parts of figure 4-2—I. Fair Market Value, II. Rental Income, III. Expenses, and IV. Net Operating Income/Cash Flow—are the areas to focus on as you begin collecting your property's data. All of these segments work together to help you analyze your properties and determine which is the better investment deal for you. Throughout the rest of stage 2, we will walk through each and explain how to collect accurate numbers for your investment analysis.

POINTS TO REMEMBER

- Whether you're buying your first or your fifteenth, nothing replaces a thorough and detailed analysis of your prospective property.

- Using the HOLD worksheet to highlight the bottom-line potential of a prospect will calm the fears of first-timers and prevent veterans from taking unwise shortcuts. Your HOLD worksheet is your trusted tool in this process.

- Take the time to check your sources and your math, and you will be in great shape to make an offer.

CHAPTER 5:
ESTIMATE THE PURCHASE PRICE

<table>
<tr><td>✓</td><td>

1. FIND
The right property for the right terms and the right price

</td></tr>
</table>

Outcome: a list of qualified investment properties from which to choose

↓

2. ANALYZE
A property to make sure the numbers and the terms make sense

- ☑ **Chapter 4**: Understand Your HOLD Worksheet
- ☐ **Chapter 5**: Estimate the Purchase Price
- ☐ **Chapter 6**: Project the Rent
- ☐ **Chapter 7**: Calculate the Costs
- ☐ **Chapter 8**: Analyze the Property

↓

Outcome: a prospect that meets your financial criteria

After reading this chapter, you will know how to:

☐ Run and drive the comps.

☐ Establish the property's fair market value (FMV).

☐ Estimate your purchase price.

HOLD WORKSHEET PART I:
DETERMINE FMV AND ESTIMATE THE PURCHASE PRICE

In part I of your HOLD worksheet, the focus is on the value of the property. Every property has three prices: the list price, fair market value, and what an investor would pay for the property. The list price is established by the seller with the help of an agent and is based on their analysis, market values, and condition of the property. Fair market value is your assessment of the current value of the property based on your analysis of recent sales and the property's condition. Another way to think of it is as the retail price—the price a typical buyer would pay for the property, and the price you'd expect an appraiser to arrive at. Every smart buyer does this calculation to justify their potential offer. The purchase price for an investor will virtually always fall below fair market value. Remember, investors make their money going in.

This isn't a fairness issue, nor is it an integrity issue. It's about finding value. Investors make their money by solving problems others can't or are unwilling to solve. Some properties require extensive repairs, while others require a quick or complex closing. And sometimes, because they have become experts on their target market, the investor can simply see value that others miss.

In any case, as you've learned, the HOLD investment game is about finding and acquiring cash-flow properties at value prices. The first step on that journey is to establish the list price, fair market value, and your estimated purchase price for your HOLD worksheet.

The list price is almost always public information. After all, the seller has likely advertised the home for sale with an agent on the multiple listing service or, in some cases, themselves as a for sale by owner or FSBO. In some situations, you may identify a property you want to purchase that isn't currently for sale. Nothing prevents a savvy investor from making an offer on a desirable property. And, sometimes, people who *need* to sell will even seek you out. In those cases, you'll simply skip list price and focus on fair market value and your investor's purchase price.

In order to establish these critical numbers for your HOLD worksheet, there are three steps to follow:

1. Pull the comps.

2. Drive the comps.

3. Plug in the numbers.

1. Pull the Comps

When real estate professionals talk about "comps," they are referring to comparable sales. Collecting reliable comps—along with you and your agent's market knowledge—is what informs your purchase offer and keeps you from overpaying for a property.

Comps are also essential if you plan to finance your purchase with a conventional mortgage loan. Although people often say, "In real estate, price is what a buyer and seller determine it to be," this isn't always true. Yes, through offers and negotiations the seller and buyer reach an agreement on the current value of the home. However, when the purchase is being financed, there will be another party in this conversation—the lender. As we'll discuss in "Buy," the lender will have the house appraised by a third party who will also analyze recent comparable sales. And if the house doesn't appraise, meaning the accepted offer price is higher than the appraiser's assessment, they won't approve the loan. This process usually works in the investor's favor, as it can justify a lower offer price and prevent you from accidently overpaying. All this to say gathering accurate comps is a critical step.

The best source for your comps will be your real estate agent. In addition, you can research property values online or with your tax assessor. In some markets, sales prices are available as a matter of public record. Keep in mind, the goal is a list of properties sold in your target area in the past three months arranged according to location, date of sale, construction, and condition.

For instance, using the property at 742 Evergreen Terrace, you'd want to pull comps on 3–2 single-family homes with garages in Area 7 with similar construction that measure around 1,200 square feet. Whereas, for 127 Elm Street, you would want to pull comps on duplexes in Area 7, preferably with a 2–2/2–1 setup and a carport. Ideally, the comps should also have similar features and finishes. Remember, you want to compare apples to apples and oranges to oranges. Figures 5-1 and 5-2 will show you the comps for both prospective properties, respectively.

Remember, in most cases the most recently sold homes will have the strongest bearing on what price your home should be. Three to four months' worth of sales data is ideal, but if that doesn't yield a sufficient sample, you can look back further.

Notice in both figures 5-1 and 5-2, there's a highlighted row for the average sales price, square footage, and price per square foot. This is an important step. Reducing a property to its price per square foot is a standard for real estate professionals and a part of any formal appraisal process. When you have an average price per square foot from the comps, you can then multiply that by the actual square footage of the property you're considering to get a sense of how accurately the home is priced. We'll do just that in the final step of part I.

Comparative Market Analysis for 742 Evergreen Terrace (SFH)							
Address	Price Sold	Sq. Feet	Price/ Sq. Ft.	Beds	Baths	Stories	Year Built
221 Main St.	$172,000	1,390	$124	3	2	2	1979
1644 King St.	$145,000	1,100	$132	2	1	1	1982
437 Euclid Dr.	$189,000	1,715	$110	4	2	2	1986
1214 Highland Ave.	$170,000	1,400	$121	3	2	1	1970
26 Evergreen Terr.	$157,900	1,300	$121	3	2	1	1975
13 Elm St.	$169,900	1,460	$116	3	1	1	1981
137 Main St.	$185,000	1,500	$123	4	2	1	1980
279 Evergreen Terr.	$155,000	1,100	$141	3	1	1	1973
115 Euclid Dr.	$142,000	1,100	$129	2	1	1	1984
1789 Main St.	$160,000	1,150	$139	3	2	1	1979
Average	$164,580	1,321	$125				
742 Evergreen Terr.		1,200		3	2	1	1984

Figure 5-1

Comparative Market Analysis for 127 Elm Street (Duplex)

Address	Price Sold	Sq. Feet	Price/ Sq. Ft.	Beds	Baths	Stories	Year Built
345 Main St.	$230,000	1,770	$130	2 2	2 1	1	1979
189 Elm St.	$195,000	1,475	$132	2 1	1 1	1	1982
1234 Euclid Dr.	$240,900	2,000	$120	3 2	2 1	1	1986
278 Highland Ave.	$210,000	1,800	$117	2 1	2 1	1	1970
76 Evergreen Terr.	$205,900	2,100	$98	2 1	1 1	1	1975
342 Elm St.	$229,900	1,700	$135	2 2	2 2	1	1981
198 Main St.	$215,000	1,800	$119	3 1	2 1	1	1980
334 Evergreen Terr.	$200,000	1,500	$133	2 1	2 2	1	1973
879 Euclid Dr.	$198,000	1,650	$120	2 2	1 1	1	1984
237 Main St.	$217,000	1,400	$155	2 1	1 1	1	1979
Average	$214,170	1,719	**$125**				
127 Elm Street		**1,640**		2 2	2 1	1	1979

Figure 5-2

If the local city council in conjunction with a neighborhood development board determines that an area is ready for revitalization, there may be incentive programs for investors. These might include tax benefits, community development block grants with special financing, county bond programs, and other government programs to encourage people to buy or fix up properties in that area. Knowing how to pull and analyze comps will help you understand potential investment properties in your target market. But looking at a table is not enough to complete a proper analysis. Once you have the comps, you must drive them.

2. Drive the Comps

Comparing the numbers is vital to understanding where your leads stand in the market, but it doesn't take into account such variables as the home's current condition or whether the house is in a desirable location. Your real estate agent can help you decide whether your prospects are well priced, but it's always smart to get in your car and "drive the comps" to see for yourself how your target property measures up to the competition.

You'll want to look at elements that are more difficult to quantify but could add or detract from a home's value. The "soft" features to consider include curb appeal, the property's overall condition, and condition of the neighborhood. If one home is well kept and others around it are in shambles, it'll be more challenging to make an accurate comparison. Other things you'll want to look for are neighborhood amenities, school systems, and traffic. Is the home on a busy street or next to a freeway?

It's not uncommon to have what looks like the "perfect comp" on paper only to discover it should be eliminated altogether because the "fixer-up" is falling apart, or it has a utility easement cutting through the middle of the "unique backyard." Nothing replaces driving the comps so that you can accurately assess your comparable sales properties. Some may need to be discounted, increased, or eliminated altogether.

For our target properties on Evergreen Terrace and Elm Street, your comps turned out to be accurate.

3. Plug in the Numbers

Your agent pulled the comps in figures 5-1 and 5-2 for both 742 Evergreen Terrace and 127 Elm Street in Springfield. He found that comparable single-family homes in Area 7 sold in the past three months had an average purchase price of $164,580, or $125/sq. ft., and comparable duplexes went for $214,170, or again $125/sq. ft.

Having established the average price per square foot for both prospects, we now need to estimate their fair market value. To do this, you multiply the actual square footage of your property by the average price per square foot of the comps. For example, 742 Evergreen Terrace is 1,200 square feet and 1,200 times an average price per square foot of $125 yields an estimated fair market value of $150,000.

742 Evergreen Terrace Fair Market Value

1,200 sq. ft. x $125 = $150,000

Figure 5-3

This actually lines up perfectly with the listing price, which, though unusual, isn't unheard of. If the property is priced right, it may mean the seller is motivated to sell quickly and the listing agent has done a good job of pricing the property correctly. Doing the same math on the duplex on Elm Street yields a more typical result.

127 Elm Street Fair Market Value

1,640 sq. ft. x $125 = $205,000

Figure 5-4

This is below the list price of $210,000, but because you have reviewed and even driven your comps, you feel confident in your assessment. With fair market value in hand, you can now start filling in the blanks on your HOLD worksheet. The first is your discount ...

Figures 5-5 and 5-6 are what the top portion—part I—of your two property worksheets should look like purchased on a 30-year note. As we mentioned earlier, we included the median interest rate for the United States on a 30-year note over the last thirty years—6.94 percent. You'll also notice we've left the current list prices for each Springfield property as is, since in pulling the comps we found both properties to be within fair market value.

As noted in "Find," savvy investors look, on average, for a discount rate of at least 10 percent, and go in looking to put 25 percent down. So, we used these target marks as our numbers in both property assessments. Remember, these are good target percentage rates when shopping for an investment property in the median-level purchase price range. However, again, you'll want to consult your HOLD team, local market trends, and your own criteria to help you arrive at your maximum offer price.

HOLD Property Analysis Worksheet - SFH

Prepared By _____ Client Name _____

Property Address: 742 Evergreen Terrace **List Price: $150,000**

Fair Market Value: $150,000

Discount (%,$)	10%	$15,000.00
Purchase Price (max offer price)	**$135,000.00**	
Percent Down	25%	
Down Payment Amount	**$33,750.00**	
Amount Financed	**$101,250.00**	
Interest Rate	6.94%	
Costs of Repairs (make-ready)	$11,000.00	
Length of Mortgage (years)	30	

	Monthly	Annual
Mortgage Payment	**$669.54**	**$8,034.53**

Figure 5-5

HOLD Property Analysis Worksheet - Duplex

Prepared By _____ Client Name _____

Property Address: 127 Elm Street **List Price: $210,000**

Fair Market Value: $205,000

Discount (%,$)	10%	$20,500.00
Purchase Price (max offer price)	**$184,500.00**	
Percent Down	25%	
Down Payment Amount	**$46,125.00**	
Amount Financed	**$138,375.00**	
Interest Rate	6.94%	
Costs of Repairs (make-ready)	$11,000.00	
Length of Mortgage (years)	30	

	Monthly	Annual
Mortgage Payment	**$915.04**	**$10,980.52**

Figure 5-6

In this case, notice a 10 percent discount will give you $15,000 off 742 Evergreen Terrace, and $20,500 off of 127 Elm Street. These amounts subtracted from the fair market value of each property determine your first estimated maximum offer price—$135,000 and $184,500, respectively.

When all these numbers are plugged in, we arrive at your monthly and annual mortgage payment for each property. According to the worksheet, in the single-family purchase, you'll pay about $669.54 monthly or a little more than $8,000 annually. Whereas the duplex monthly payment equals out to be $915.04, or approximately $11,000 a year. These numbers are important to watch and readjust as necessary during your analysis to make sure your investment cash flows and meets your financial criteria. Finally, you'll note in figures 5-5 and 5-6 that there is a row for "Costs of Repairs." While we won't cover that number until Chapter 7: Calculate the Costs, we can address why it appears here. A big factor in any investment property acquisition is the cash needed to close. Your down payment will likely be your largest single cost. However, the second-largest cost can often be for repairs needed to make the property available for rent. Investors often refer to these as "make-ready" repairs. We chose to position these costs in close proximity to the down payment, so you can quickly add up the total out-of-pocket cash requirements on any potential investment transaction.

The next step in the Analyze process is to project monthly rental incomes for each property.

POINTS TO REMEMBER

- Your investor purchase price is key in the HOLD strategy, and properly collecting and running the numbers in part I of your worksheet will help you arrive at an estimate you can feel confident in.

- Follow the three simple steps mentioned in chapter 5—pull the comps, drive the comps, and plug in the numbers—to determine your list price, fair market value, and investor purchase price, and you will have a solid base to continue your analysis.

CHAPTER 6: PROJECT THE RENT

> ✓ **1. FIND**
> The right property for the right terms and the right price

Outcome: a list of qualified investment properties from which to choose

↓

2. ANALYZE
A property to make sure the numbers and the terms make sense
- ☑ **Chapter 4**: Understand Your HOLD Worksheet
- ☑ **Chapter 5**: Estimate the Purchase Price
- ☐ **Chapter 6**: Project the Rent
- ☐ **Chapter 7**: Calculate the Costs
- ☐ **Chapter 8**: Analyze the Property

↓

Outcome: a prospect that meets your financial criteria

After reading this chapter, you will know how to:

☐ Collect the comps.

☐ Project the rent.

COLLECT THE COMPS

Projecting rents is a very important step in the Analyze process, as it determines your income and cash flow for prospective properties. If you project too high, you could be stuck with a vacant property or one with a negative cash flow. Conversely, if you project too low, your numbers may not calculate in your favor, and you could walk away from a great deal.

So, to alleviate these worries, again refer to your HOLD worksheets, and much like the comparative market analysis we walked through in chapter 5, you'll complete a similar search to find actual rental comps in your neighborhood. You're again looking for comparable properties near your prospect to get a handle on average monthly and annual rental incomes. Knowing the current rental values for comps is essential to accurately project the rents for your property. So, there are four resources we suggest you tap to pull rental comps:

1. Multiple Listing Service (MLS)

2. Property Managers

3. Local Listings (Newspaper and Online)

4. Area Rental Signs

1. Multiple Listing Service (MLS)

You can find rental income rates from a number of sources, but the No. 1 place to get the information is from the MLS. Why? Two reasons: First, the MLS is operated and maintained by real estate professionals with ethics and standards enforced. You can generally trust the numbers.

Second, while most databases show what is currently advertised for rent, with the help of your real estate agent, you can often pull actual rental histories for properties. Besides giving you historical perspective, this can be important in shifting markets. In a "hot market," the advertised rents may be lower than the actuals if the landlord has multiple applicants. Conversely, in a "cold market," advertised rents may be higher than actuals if the landlord has to negotiate. The MLS can lead you closer to the truth in both cases.

A quick glance at a listing will show the asking price, square footage, number of bedrooms, age of the property, and its amenities. However, as your agent will show you, oftentimes you can see what your competition requires of applicants: how much they're charging for a security, pet, or cleaning deposit, and if a credit or background check is required.

You can search for properties that have been newly leased in the past three months. This will tell you how much a property owner is asking in monthly rent for a property like yours, and how long it was on the market before a tenant was found. Many times a thorough listing agent will include the original asking price on top of what rate it leased for.

Again, these numbers are all based on your prospect's comps. Not only will they help you approximate your rental income going in, they will help you determine if you can increase the rent costs moving forward and by how much. Be careful to make sure the numbers you use come from properties that are similar to your prospective purchase in style, size, and location. It is also important to compare at least three other properties. The more comps you can obtain, the more accurate your estimate of rents will be.

2. Property Managers

An experienced property manager can be a wealth of information and will have their fingers on the pulse of the marketplace. They can tell you which property types are getting the most inquiries, and which command the highest rents. They can keep you clear of blocks with high vacancy rates and direct you toward neighborhoods with rentals that receive multiple offers whenever there's an opening.

Your real estate agent may be able to suggest property managers you can add to your network because many are affiliated with real estate companies. Look for property managers with enough investments in their portfolios to represent market trends. The more properties they manage, the broader their perspective will be. It's important to know what kind of properties they specialize in and how many they manage. Some may have more of a focus on multifamily, while others may have more single-family homes in their portfolio. Once you connect with a property manager, these key questions will elicit the kind of information you'll need to get an accurate picture of the rental market in your target neighborhood.

It is, however, important to remember that if you are not going to be using a property manager to help maintain the investment, you may be better off talking to other local investors who maintain their own properties. Property managers do this for a living. So, while they can provide a wealth of info for their clients to work with, they may not be keen to share information on an ongoing basis for free.

What to Ask a Property Manager

1. Which property types are renting quickly?
2. What rents are you getting for a typical three-bedroom home?
3. How long are the homes in this area on the market?
4. What is the vacancy factor right now?
5. Are rents going up or down?
6. Are you offering any concessions for a new renter or lease renewal?
7. How many single-family homes do you manage?
8. How many multifamily properties?
9. What amenities must a property have to rent quickly?

Figure 6-1

3. Local Listings (Newspaper and Online)

The Internet is a great source for rental information. In fact, it's becoming more and more popular for buyers to shop for an apartment online through a rental listing service like Craigslist.org or Rentals.com. Other sites like SpeedyTenants.com are fantastic places to get a general feel for what's going on in the rental market.

Of course, the local newspaper and its companion website are still go-to resources for real estate. Landlords who don't use property managers will often list their rentals here. Some newspaper websites are linked to other online resources like Apartments.com, where you'll find large apartment complexes with a sprinkling of single-family homes. Both are good places to shop the local rental market and scope your competition.

4. Area Rental Signs

Lastly, don't forget to drive your target neighborhood looking for rental signs. Some may have fliers that list basic information about the property, including the rental rate and whether it includes utilities and other household bills. Most will have just a phone number on the "For Rent" sign, so you'll have to call to get this info.

Driving the area for unlisted rentals can be invaluable for pricing. If there are four duplexes a block over from your prospect renting for less, it will have a real impact on your finances. Whereas home buyers can fall in love with a property, renters tend to look for value. Overpricing your rental by even $100 per month could cost you weeks of lost income as the property sits vacant.

Applying this to our hypothetical, let's say in your research for the single-family at 742 Evergreen Terrace you found eight recent comps. But, when you drove the area, you eliminated five because they didn't measure up in real life. You also added one additional unadvertised rental on Euclid Drive. Now you're left with four reliable comps to help narrow your projected rental income for a single family with no prior rental history.

HOLD WORKSHEET PART II: PROJECT THE RENTS

If you still think you may have found a winner once you've driven the comps (collected in figure 6-2), the next thing you need to do is settle on a rental income for your properties.

Comparative Rental Income Market Analysis for 742 Evergreen Terrace (SFH)

Address	Rent	Sq. Feet	Rent/ Sq. Ft.	Beds	Baths	Stories	Year Built
137 Main St.	$1,560	1,600	$0.98	4	2	1	1980
279 Evergreen Terr.	$1,380	1,100	$1.25	3	1	1	1973
115 Euclid Dr.	$1,225	900	$1.36	2	1	1	1984
1789 Main St.	$1,400	1,200	$1.17	3	2	1	1979
Average	$1,391	1,200	$1.16				
742 Evergreen Terr.		**1,200**					

Figure 6-2

The projected rental income will drive the second part of your HOLD worksheet and play a large part in determining if your prospect will cash flow or not. Not to worry—based on figure 6-2, it's an easy four-step process to determine your projection number.

1. Find the Average Monthly Rental Income

As you can see in figure 6-2, the monthly rents of the comparable properties you collected run from $1,225 to $1,560. The average monthly rental income of these four is $1,391. This number is an important base, but you'll need to break it down by square foot and rent per square foot to find an accurate projection.

2. Find the Average Square Footage of the Comps

As discussed in step one, your end goal is to find an average rental price per square foot based on comparable properties currently renting in the neighborhood. Since we've already determined the average monthly rental income of our four comps, we can now find the average square footage. As figure 6-2 shows, that number is 1,200 square feet.

3. Calculate the Average Rent Per Square Foot

Using the averages you found in steps one and two, you can easily figure the average rent per square foot currently being charged in your target location. Simply divide the average monthly rental income by the average square footage. In this case it will be $1,391/1,200 sq. ft. or $1.16 a square foot.

4. Project Your Rent

Now that you've arrived at an average rental price per square foot, you can easily project your prospect's rent. 742 Evergreen Terrace is 1,200 square feet, and your average rent per square foot is $1.16. That being said, your projected rental income for the single-family property is 1,200 multiplied by $1.16, or $1,392.

742 Evergreen Terrace Rent Projection

1,200 sq. ft. x $1.16 = $1,392/month

Figure 6-3

To make this a more even number, we're going to suggest you round it to the nearest $10 increment. Let's project your single-family property's rent at $1,390. You'll see this is the projected rent in part II of your worksheet—shown in figure 6-4—and will be the income estimate we use for the rest of the property analysis.

HOLD Property Analysis Worksheet - SFH		

Prepared By _____   Client Name _____

Property Address: 742 Evergreen Terrace

Rental Income	Monthly	Annual
Unit A	$ 1,390.00	$ 16,680.00
Unit B	$ --	$ --
Unit C	$ --	$ --
Unit D	$ --	$ --
Gross Rental Income	$ 1,390.00	$ 16,680.00
Vacancy Rate	5.0 %	5.0 %
Net Rental Income	**$ 1,320.50**	**$ 15,846.00**

Figure 6-4

Since the duplex at 127 Elm Street currently has tenants in both units, you can start with those numbers as your ballpark in your analysis of that property. However, we encourage you to complete the same exercise for all prospective properties, including those with current tenants. Leases can end for several reasons, and to help minimize vacancy rates, you'll want to know what the market comps are on the duplex as well.

For the duplex, we are assuming you've done the same due diligence to ensure the current rents are at worst below market, and we've decided to use those numbers for units A and B in figure 6-5.

HOLD Property Analysis Worksheet - Duplex

Prepared By _____   Client Name _____

Property Address: 127 Elm Street

Rental Income	Monthly	Annual
Unit A	$ 1,125.00	$ 13,500.00
Unit B	$ 850.00	$ 10,200.00
Unit C	$ --	$ --
Unit D	$ --	$ --
Gross Rental Income	$ 1,975.00	$ 23,700.00
Vacancy Rate	5.0 %	5.0 %
Net Rental Income	**$ 1,876.25**	**$ 22,515.00**

Figure 6-5

As you can see in figures 6-4 and 6-5, after collecting rental comps and inputting a monthly rental income estimate, you'll need to account for vacancy. For our purposes, we're going to suggest you assume a 5 percent vacancy rate which would translate to about 18 or 19 days a year that you don't get rent. This is a handy rule of thumb but your actual vacancy rates will be determined by the rents you charge, the condition of your property, and the amount of competition you face. Even the time of year can have an impact. Talk to your HOLD team for relevent info on your specific property and your market. Figure 6-4 verifies after subtracting $69.50 per month to cover your annual vacancy rate, your projected net monthly rental income for 742 Evergreen Terrace is $1,320.50. Similarly, after combining Unit A and B's projected monthly rents, you can see 127 Elm Street grosses $1,975 per month in figure 6-5. And when you subtract the suggested 5 percent vacancy, your projected net rental income on the duplex is $1,876.25.

POINTS TO REMEMBER

- The Analyze phase of the HOLD strategy is key, and spending the extra time and energy to collect accurate numbers for your analysis worksheet will pay you back immensely in the end.

- Don't be afraid to ask for help. Numbers do not come naturally to everyone, but that's what the HOLD worksheet and your trusted investment team are there for—to help you make the best investment decisions along your wealth-building journey.

- Remember to keep "cash flow is king" top of mind.

- Cash Flow = Net Operating Income – Debt Service (Mortgage Payment)

CHAPTER 7: CALCULATE THE COSTS

✓	**1. FIND** **The right property for the right terms and the right price**

Outcome: a list of qualified investment properties from which to choose

↓

2. ANALYZE
A property to make sure the numbers and the terms make sense

☑ **Chapter 4**: Understand Your HOLD Worksheet

☑ **Chapter 5**: Estimate the Purchase Price

☑ **Chapter 6**: Project the Rent

☐ **Chapter 7**: Calculate the Costs

☐ **Chapter 8**: Analyze the Property

↓

Outcome: a prospect that meets your financial criteria

After reading this chapter, you will know how to:

☐ Estimate your expenses.

☐ Understand how financing affects your investment's value.

☐ Estimate your cost of repairs.

HOLD WORKSHEET PART III: ESTIMATE YOUR EXPENSES

There are several expenses you need to take into account to properly analyze your prospective properties. These have been outlined in part III of the HOLD Property Analysis Worksheet, as you can see below. There are seven line items that need to be analyzed: property management fees, leasing costs, maintenance reserve, utilities, property taxes, insurance, and a catchall we creatively named "other." We're going to walk through each of these separately and provide guidelines for how to project these costs in part III, seen in figures 7-1 and 7-2 as we go.

We're going to begin with all of the blanks filled in for you according to our suggested methods. As you go through each step in this chapter, feel free to refer back to figures 7-1 and 7-2 as frequently as you need for visual reinforcement.

HOLD Property Analysis Worksheet - SFH

Prepared By _____   Client Name _____

Property Address: 742 Evergreen Terrace

Expenses	Monthly	Annual
Property Management Fees	$132.05	$1,584.60
Leasing Costs	$57.92	$695.04
Maintenance Reserve	$66.03	$792.36
Utilities	$0	$0
Property Taxes	$250.00	$3,000.00
Insurance	$62.50	$750.00
Other (HOA fees, lawn care, trash, etc.)	$15.00	$180.00
Total Expenses	**$583.50**	**$7,002.00**

Figure 7-1

HOLD Property Analysis Worksheet - Duplex

Prepared By _____   Client Name _____

Property Address: 127 Elm Street

Expenses	Monthly	Annual
Property Management Fees	$187.63	$2,251.50
Leasing Costs	$82.29	$987.48
Maintenance Reserve	$93.81	$1,125.72
Utilities	$0	$0
Property Taxes	$341.67	$4,100.04
Insurance	$85.42	$1,025.04
Other (HOA fees, lawn care, trash, etc.)	$15.00	$180.00
Total Expenses	**$805.82**	**$9,669.78**

Figure 7-2

1. Property Management Fees

Property managers are usually paid from your collected rents. They typically will collect the rents for you and take a percentage off the top. So they only get paid when you do. Historically, property managers charge 10 percent of the annual net rental income, although costs vary from market to market. Call a few recommended property managers to discover the going rate in your area. Make sure to ask for a list of all the charges—some may charge a lower percentage, but there will be other fees to consider.

Hiring a property manager is a choice. Managing the residence yourself may save you several hundred dollars a year. Just understand, you are trading your time for these savings. While self-management can be a great learning experience for investors, it isn't for everyone. If you opt to go it alone, be sure to get expert advice where needed, including researching the local and state laws regarding landlord/tenant requirements.

To be on the safe side, we've gone ahead and filled in a common percentage of net rent after vacancy for both Springfield prospects in figures 7-1 and 7-2—a monthly cost of $132.05 and $187.63, respectively. As a general rule of thumb, we like to do our analysis with property management costs included—even when we plan to manage it ourselves. Your circumstances can change quickly, and you'll be thankful you included these costs should you decide to hire a property manager down the line.

2. Leasing Costs

When it comes to leasing costs, there is no rule of thumb, but there are three options:

I.   Lease by yourself.

II. List with a real estate agent.

III. Leverage a property manager.

This expense will vary greatly depending on how you list the property for rent. Do-it-yourself (DIY) is the least expensive, but it may cost you time. Agents typically charge around 50 percent of one month's rent to show and lease your property. As mentioned above, a property manager will take a percentage of net rents for the duration of your lease, and may pass along some added costs.

Our philosophy is budget for the worst-case scenarios. That means we're encouraging you to use the most costly—list with an agent—as your model, which would be about 50 percent of one month's rent. In your

Springfield properties, this ends up being $695.04 for the single-family home, and $987.48 for the duplex, as you can see in figures 7-1 and 7-2 on pp. 82-83. These onetime leasing costs should be saved for throughout the year (about $57 and $82 a month for the respective properties) so you never have to write a big check.

3. Maintenance Reserve

Your maintenance reserve is money set aside for parts and labor when something breaks, needs a tune-up, or must be upgraded. It is meant to accumulate over time as a sort of "emergency fund," so that even if you have no major fixes in the first five years, come year six when part of the roof needs to be replaced, you will already have the money to do so.

Though it is tied closely to property management, maintenance reserve is broken out separately, as property management is largely paid on a monthly basis for someone else's time and for basic upkeep—lawn mowing, bush trimming, etc. Your reserve is for annual fixes that may range from paint or carpet replacement when a tenant leaves to fixing your HVAC system.

When it comes to maintenance, a good rule of thumb is to save 3 to 6 percent of the property's annual net rental income. Of course some things to consider when deciding on a percentage are the home's age and how "nice" you'd like to keep the property. Older homes may require larger-scale maintenance and a higher reserve. Conversely, if you simply want to keep your property in pristine shape to minimize vacancy and maximize rents, you may need to bump up the expense to 10 percent. The good news is that once you establish a healthy reserve, say enough to cover a replaced roof or HVAC, you can opt to stop setting this money aside.

For the two hypotheticals, we chose to err on the more conservative side of the norm, at 5 percent—$66.03 for the single-family and $93.81 for the duplex—as noted in figures 7-1 and 7-2.

4. Utilities

Buying a residential rental property as an investment means that utilities will, for the most part, be paid by your tenant any way you slice it. Since some residential properties are zoned for commercial use (say a house that could occupy a beauty salon or other small business), we've kept it in our worksheet.

For a single-family home and duplexes, the utilities will simply be put in the tenant's name and turned off only if there is a vacancy. We've added $15 a month into the "other" expenses category for that rare occurrence when you must activate the utilities in your name. With larger multifamilies, there is often a shared meter cost passed on to the tenants. Depending on how well you project the utility costs, this can keep your expense low or even turn a small profit.

5. Property Taxes

Taxes are another expense that will vary widely depending on where your property is located. For instance: country vs. city, amount of land, inland vs. coastal, population, etc. But, states with no income tax will have a higher property tax.

In 2009 the United States' low was in Louisiana at 0.14 percent of property value, and the high was in Texas at 1.76 percent. For an average-priced home ($170,000), that's a $2,754 a year difference.

As you'll recall in figures 7-1 and 7-2 on pp. 82-83, we again have erred on the conservative side, estimating 742 Evergreen Terrace's property tax at 2 percent as $3,000, and 127 Elm Street's as $4,100.

6. Insurance

Home insurance is extremely important. Your home as well as your investment properties are some of your greatest assets. So why wouldn't you insure them?

In fact, if you purchase your property on a conventional loan, your lender will require you to insure the property. After all, if you default, they get the asset including the insurance value as if it were destroyed by a fire, flood, or other disaster.

A great place to start when looking for rates is with your own insurance agent if you own a car, motorcycle, boat, or the like. Many insurers give better deals to policyholders with multiple—car, home, life, etc.—insured items. Your agent should be able to quickly give you a quote.

However, before you readily accept the first offer, do a little of your own research to decide on a price point to insure. We recommend insuring at least your home's estimated replacement cost. A rule of thumb to estimate insurance costs is half a percent of the property's fair market value. For your Evergreen Terrace prospect, that comes out to be $750 a year or $62.50 a month. For Elm Street, insurance will likely cost you $1,025.04 or and $85.42 a month. Keep in mind, insurance companies want your business, so realize it isn't much hassle getting a quote—or several for that matter.

7. Other

The final category in part III of your HOLD worksheet is all-encompassing and therefore termed "other." This is where you will put aside any extra cash you need to save for unexpected, uncommon, or added expenses. As we discussed earlier, we've already set aside $15 a month for each prospective property in our hypothetical to cover unexpected utility fees.

Another more common expense in this category might be homeowners association (HOA) fees. These are fees tied to a legal entity created to maintain specific neighborhoods and communities. Typically, HOA fees are tied to condominiums, town houses, or newer single-family subdivisions, but it is very important to verify for each of your prospects, as monthly dues can range extensively.

Total Your Expenses

Now that you've walked through and been meticulous in estimating each line item in part III of your HOLD worksheet, it's time to add them. When you look back at figures 7-1 and 7-2 on pp. 82-83, you'll see that total expense costs for your single-family are estimated to be $583.50 a month or $7,002 annually. Meanwhile, your duplex estimates add up to $805.82 a month or $9,669.78 in year one. These totals are important, as they play into part IV of your worksheet and will help you determine net operating income and cash flow.

ESTIMATE FINANCING COSTS

There are a number of ways to tackle the cost of financing and many types of loans available that will have an impact on long-term vs. short-term investments. For instance, some investors who have more cash to put down up front opt to buy down the interest rates. This is when you pay a larger sum to your lender to decrease the rate on the remainder of your mortgage. Of course, we urge you to discuss all of your options with your lender prior to making any financial decisions around interest. And, we will discuss several options in more detail during the Buy phase of your HOLD journey.

Smart investors who own a number of properties learn to play the mortgage game with skill and careful research. They keep an eye on the ever-evolving mortgage market, watch for new loan offerings that would be attractive or useful for investors, and understand how their personal finances can impact the loans and interest rates available to them.

Granted, mortgage financing may seem a bit daunting at first, but over time you'll master financing. You'll either personally become an expert or, more likely, develop a working relationship with a mortgage professional who will keep you informed. Your ultimate goal here is to understand and capitalize on the inner workings of the mortgage market to maximize your profits over time.

A good place to start is your own financial criteria. Based on this, you'll automatically analyze your properties with a bias toward one financing method or another. For example, investors interested in excelled equity buildup usually opt for 15-year notes, while those looking for a longer journey with higher immediate cash flow look to 30-year options. There are many financing possibilities out there, so start with your criteria.

Sticking to your criteria will help alert you to properties that may not be a good fit. Sure, there will always be other financial options, or as many call it "creative financing," but we do not suggest this be the first place you go when your financial criteria is not met. We'll discuss these options further in the Buy segment. For now, remember this: Don't force it. Just because you can find a way doesn't mean you should.

For our analysis of the Springfield properties, we're going to use the most common choice among home buyers—a 30-year note—and compare it to a 15-year note for our analysis. Again, we'll be using 30-year median mortgage interest rates for both.

KNOW YOUR COST OF REPAIRS

Your cost of repairs is the final number to consider when analyzing a property. Though it will not be a monthly expense, it will affect the numbers going in and influence your decision to purchase and even your offer price. Knowing the cost of repairs will help you make an offer that is fair to the seller and profitable for you.

It's important to recognize that almost all investment properties will need some repair work. After all, this is often why you are able to get them at such a discount. Just remember, you may need to put a bit more into make-ready repairs up front so that you can quickly rent the property at its highest value. This is nearly always specific to a property, so it is difficult to estimate. However, remaining on the safe side of the fence, we are going to account for the higher end of what make-ready repairs would look like on an investment property. The checklist in figure 7-3 will help you start thinking about repairs that may need to get done quickly after purchase, and how much you might spend.

Cost of Possible Make-Ready Repairs		
	Low-Mid	Mid-High
Flooring	$1,500	$2,000
Paint – Interior	$1,000	$1,500
Paint – Exterior	$1,000	$1,500
Replace HVAC	$5,000	$5,500
Re-key	$100	$100
Cleaning	$100	$100
Landscaping	$250	$350
Misc. Repairs	$500	$500
Misc. Fixtures	$500	$500
Total Expenses	**$9,950**	**$12,050**
Average	**$11,000**	

Figure 7-3

Many of these repairs are quick cosmetic facelifts—paint, flooring, fixtures, etc. However, you may also have to do some more extensive repairs in year one. For instance, if the house is older, it may need some electrical work, or a new roof or HVAC unit. These costs will be a onetime expense going in, and then you hopefully won't need to revisit them for some time. Getting a thorough list of needed repairs with cost estimates is a vital step in the Analyze process, and will usually give you some leeway to negotiate price with the seller, as well.

Notice the make-ready totals in figure 7-3 average to be about $11,000. That's a conservatively high amount we've used—remember, from part III of our HOLD Property Analysis Worksheet. It's always better to meet your property and financial criteria at the $11,000 estimate and be pleasantly surprised when you only need to spend $5,000 on make-ready repairs.

But to try and make your list as accurate as possible, plan to spend some time at the property, take pictures of anything you have questions about or want to repair, get cost estimates from contractors, and, to a certain degree, trust your gut. Yes, we always suggest consulting an expert, but many properties will be visibly in need of repairs. Talk to your agent, and even do local research to see what said repairs might cost.

Keep in mind, the cost of repairs is important for several reasons. First, a property's condition often affects the rent it can generate. This can add paper value to your investment. Second, the number also represents cash in the deal, and cash is the ultimate commodity when buying an investment. As a smart investor, you should balance your desire to give your property a top-of-the-line finish-out with the understanding that all the money you save on repairs can be invested in another property.

In fact, many investors follow a "make-ready formula" that reflects the renters they want to attract. For instance, how you finish out a vacation rental will differ from the improvements you make to a home in a working-class, family-oriented neighborhood. Price out repairs that are appropriate for your target market. And don't confuse "thrifty" with "cheap." Smart HOLD investors "bullet proof" their properties by investing in quality, durable, onetime repairs and upgrades that will survive many tenants.

POINTS TO REMEMBER

There are key numbers you need to collect before you can analyze a property (which we'll do in the next chapter). Doing your due diligence first will pay off in the end, so let's run through the numbers:

- **Purchase Price:** After you pull the comps, you drive them to get a true estimate of fair market value. Based on this number and your goal discount, you should arrive at an estimated purchase price where you'll make money going in.

- **Rental Income:** You can find rental comps in your property's neighborhood through several sources: the MLS, property managers, local online and print listings, and area rental signs. Project a fair rental income, as it can severely affect your cash flow. And remember to include vacancy rates.

- **Expenses:** When estimating your expenses, there is a lot to consider—property management fees, leasing costs, maintenance, utilities, property taxes, insurance, and others. Aside from doing due diligence on each of those, comprising an accurate cost of repairs and a financing solution that works are musts.

- **Net Operating Income and Cash Flow:** These are the final numbers added to your HOLD worksheet in part IV. In the next chapter, we will walk through how to calculate both, and then use your completed HOLD Property Analysis Worksheet to analyze the Springfield properties.

CHAPTER 8: ANALYZE THE PROPERTY

> ✓ | **1. FIND**
> The right property for the right terms and the right price

Outcome: a list of qualified investment properties from which to choose

↓

> **2. ANALYZE**
> A property to make sure the numbers and the terms make sense
> ☑ **Chapter 4**: Understand Your HOLD Worksheet
> ☑ **Chapter 5**: Estimate the Purchase Price
> ☑ **Chapter 6**: Project the Rent
> ☑ **Chapter 7**: Calculate the Costs
> ☐ **Chapter 8**: Analyze the Property

↓

Outcome: a prospect that meets your financial criteria

After reading this chapter, you will know how to:

☐ Calculate your net operating income (NOI) and determine your cash flow.

☐ Analyze your prospects.

☐ Use Analysis quick tricks.

HOLD WORKSHEET PART IV:
CALCULATE YOUR NOI AND DETERMINE CASH FLOW

Now that you have parts I, II, and III of the HOLD worksheet filled out for 742 Evergreen Terrace and 127 Elm Street, let's do the math in part IV to calculate your net operating income (NOI) on each property. Remember, your NOI is all the income you make on your property after expenses, but not including your mortgage payment. This is an important number to estimate correctly, as it will play a large part in your investment decision. You will use this number to determine if your prospect cash flows or not.

Figure 8-1 shows the tried-and-true formula for predicting your net operating income on both Springfield properties:

Net Operating Income (NOI) = Net Rental Income (NRI) – Expenses
(not including mortgage)

Notice again, we are working with both properties on a 30-year note in our hypothetical to alleviate any muddying of the waters during your initial estimate of the numbers. Later in this chapter, you will get to explore other scenarios—including purchasing on a 15-year note—during the individual property analysis.

Calculate Your Monthly NOI on a 30-Year Note		
	742 Evergreen Terrace	**127 Elm Street**
30-Year NRI	$1,320.50	$1,876.25
Expenses	-$583.50	-$805.81
30-Year NOI	**$737.00**	**$1,070.44**

Figure 8-1

As you can see, your net operating income on the duplex is about $350 more a month than on the single-family home. Awesome? Yes. Purchase decision made? Not even close. Don't worry, after you determine if the properties cash flow, you get to play in the Analyze phase. But first, you need to calculate cash flow.

Now that you've determined a monthly net operating income of $737.00 for 742 Evergreen Terrace, and $1,070.44 for 127 Elm Street, you can do the math to see if your properties cash flow by subtracting your mortgage payment from your net operating income:

Cash Flow = Net Operating Income – Debt Service (Mortgage Payment)

HOLD Property Analysis Worksheet - SFH

Property Address: 742 Evergreen Terrace

	Monthly	Annual
Net Operating Income	$737.00	$8,844.00
Mortgage Payment	$669.54	$8,034.53
Net Cash Flow	**$67.46**	**$809.47**

Figure 8-2

HOLD Property Analysis Worksheet - Duplex

Property Address: 127 Elm Street

	Monthly	Annual
Net Operating Income	$1,070.44	$12,845.30
Mortgage Payment	$915.04	$10,980.52
Net Cash Flow	**$155.40**	**$1,864.78**

Figure 8-3

In figures 8-2 and 8-3, you'll see that both prospective Springfield properties do indeed cash flow on a 30-year note with your estimates. Again, the duplex cash flows more than double the single-family's take-home. But the most exciting part is they are both in the black. Congratulations! This is another triumphant moment and litmus test passed—though you still cannot zero in on a decision to buy.

Now comes the fun part where you get to analyze both the single-family and duplex as an investor to make sure the numbers work.

IT'S TIME TO ANALYZE

Now that you've done your due diligence finding target investments, running and driving the comps, estimating rental income and expenses, and determining your NOI, it's time to reflect on your criteria, run the numbers, and analyze each property. This is where you get to listen to your gut, tinker with your worksheet, and evaluate your prospects top to bottom to make sure the numbers meet your HOLD investment goals.

This can again feel a bit emotion-fueled as single-family vs. duplex pros and cons are weighed, personal wealth-building goals are revisited, and large-ticket items are discussed. It's OK to have a sense of fear and excitement, but make sure the numbers settle that hesitancy and tip the scales to a smart purchase. And remember: 1. cash flow is king, and 2. make money going in.

The Pros and Cons of a Single-Family Home vs. a Duplex

Single-families and duplexes are very different investments—not only aesthetically speaking, but also financially, maintenance-wise, and management-wise. We are not here to sway your decision one way or the other. In fact, you'll find both property types have their unique pluses and may tend to be great properties for all investors—novices and experts alike. But, it is important to run through the pros and cons of each to find which investment type better suits your wealth-building journey.

Single-Family Home Pros and Cons

PROS

1. Tend to have higher appreciations.
2. Values more in line with marketplace.
3. Less management (time).
4. Can entail less stress on investor.

CONS

1. Single income stream makes prolonged vacancy painful.
2. Single income stream typically yields lower lifetime cash flows.

Figure 8-4

Duplex Pros and Cons

PROS

1. Multiple income streams typically offer increased cash flow.
2. Generally in line with SFH values.
3. Generally viewed similarly to SFH for financing.
4. Much lower chance for total vacancy.

CONS

1. Double the management.
2. Very market-by-market strategy.
3. At times located in less-desirable areas.

Figure 8-5

As you can see from figures 8-4 and 8-5, single-family investments tend to appreciate faster, retain value (homeowners and investors are interested at resale), entail less time on the management front, and can be less stressful to own. That being said, a duplex provides you with two income streams, higher cash flow, comparable financing options, and a very low chance of total vacancy at any given time.

On the other side of the coin, single-families tend to have a higher vacancy rate and provide only one stream of income, most times leading to less cash flow. And some things to consider with a duplex are the possibilities of it being harder to find (as small multifamily investments run market-to-market), it being located on a less appealing street, and it requiring double the management.

These of course are generalities we're offering as starting ground to help you arrive at your ideal investment property. Feel free to add to the lists—in fact, we encourage it—based on your personal and property criteria. Refer back to your checklists from the Find chapters, and revisit your wealth-building goals.

For the purpose of this book, we are going to keep both of our Springfield properties in the running to see how the numbers work.

Listen to the Numbers

That's right, we're going to say it again: cash flow is king, and you make your money going in. And now it's time to fiddle with the numbers to analyze your prospects based on these truths. For all intents and purposes, we're going to show you what the current completed worksheets for both hypothetical properties look like as is.

HOLD Property Analysis Worksheet - SFH

Prepared By _____   Client Name _____

Property Address: 742 Evergreen Terrace   **List Price: $150,000**

I. Fair Market Value: $150,000

Discount (%,$)	10%	$15,000.00
Purchase Price (max offer price)	**$135,000.00**	
Percent Down	**25%**	
Down Payment Amount	**$33,750.00**	
Amount Financed	**$101,250.00**	
Interest Rate	6.94%	
Costs of Repairs (make-ready)	$11,000.00	
Length of Mortgage (years)	30	
	Monthly	Annual
Mortgage Payment	**$669.54**	**$8,034.53**

II. Rental Income

	Monthly	Annual
Unit A	$1,390.00	$16,680.00
Unit B	$_____	$_____
Unit C	$_____	$_____
Unit D	$_____	$_____
Gross Rental Income	$1,390.00	$16,680.00
Vacancy Rate	5.0%	5.0%
Net Rental Income	**$1,320.50**	**$15,846.00**

III. Expenses

	Monthly	Annual
Property Management Fees	$132.05	$1,584.60
Leasing Costs	$57.92	$695.04
Maintenance Reserve	$66.03	$792.36
Utilities	$_____	$_____
Property Taxes	$250.00	$3,000.00
Insurance	$62.50	$750.00
Other (HOA fees, lawn care, trash, etc.)	$15.00	$180.00
Total Expenses	**$583.50**	**$7,002.00**

IV. Net Operating Income

Net Operating Income	**$737.00**	**$8,844.00**
Mortgage Payment	$669.54	$8,034.53
Net Cash Flow	**$67.46**	**$809.47**

Investment Analysis

Total Cash In (down payment + repairs)	$44,750
Appreciation Rate (20 yr. avg. = 4.4%)	4.4%
Rent Appreciation (20 yr. avg. = 3.1%)	3.1%

Figure 8-6

HOLD Property Analysis Worksheet - Duplex

Prepared By _____   Client Name _____

Property Address: 127 Elm Street   **List Price: $210,000**

I. Fair Market Value: $205,000

Discount (%,$)	10%	$20,500.00
Purchase Price (max offer price)	**$184,500.00**	
Percent Down	**25%**	
Down Payment Amount	**$46,125.00**	
Amount Financed	**$138,375.00**	
Interest Rate	6.94%	
Costs of Repairs (make-ready)	$11,000.00	
Length of Mortgage (years)	30	
	Monthly	Annual
Mortgage Payment	**$915.04**	**$10,980.52**

II. Rental Income

	Monthly	Annual
Unit A	$1,125.00	$13,500.00
Unit B	$850.00	$10,200.00
Unit C	$_____	$_____
Unit D	$_____	$_____
Gross Rental Income	$1,975.00	$23,700.00
Vacancy Rate	5.0%	5.0%
Net Rental Income	**$1,876.25**	**$22,515.00**

III. Expenses

	Monthly	Annual
Property Management Fees	$187.63	$2,251.50
Leasing Costs	$82.29	$987.48
Maintenance Reserve	$93.81	$1,125.72
Utilities	$_____	$_____
Property Taxes	$341.67	$4,100.04
Insurance	$85.42	$1,025.04
Other (HOA fees, lawn care, trash, etc.)	$15.00	$180.00
Total Expenses	**$805.82**	**$9,669.78**

IV. Net Operating Income

IV. Net Operating Income	**$1,070.43**	**$12,845.22**
Mortgage Payment	$915.04	$10,980.52
Net Cash Flow	**$155.39**	**$1,864.70**

Investment Analysis

Total Cash In (down payment + repairs)	$57,125.00
Appreciation Rate (20 yr. avg. = 4.4%)	4.4%
Rent Appreciation (20 yr. avg. = 3.1%)	3.1%

Figure 8-7

As we noted earlier, both of your hypothetical properties cash flow when purchased on a 30-year note. The single-family cash flows $67.46 a month or $809.47 annually, whereas the duplex cash flows nearly $155.39 a month and $1,864.64 annually. That being said, what if your property criteria was leaning you toward the single-family, but one of your personal criteria was to have the property paid off in 15 years? Or, what if the increased cash flow of the duplex is more in line with your goals, but your minimum requirement is a cash flow of at least $300 a month? This is where you play with the numbers, to make sure your prospects truly work for you. This is when you ask yourself, "Where can I adjust?"

In doing so, there are three areas we suggest you tinker with:

1. Financing
2. Purchase Price
3. Rental Income

1. Look at financing

When it comes to financing, the first point to highlight is the fact that even conventional 30- and 15-year notes' interest rates will change with time and market. For instance, in some markets you would be able to get the single-family home on Evergreen Terrace on a 15-year note at 4.3 percent, and it would still cash flow. As we mentioned earlier—and will delve into more deeply in the Buy segment—there is also creative financing to help adjust your numbers in your favor. We suggest talking to a professional, for instance your lender, to review all of your options and what's best to meet your personal wealth-building goals.

2. Adjust the purchase price

Let's say you're at the end of your analysis and you really want to get that duplex on Elm Street, but one of your criteria is to only purchase on 15-year notes. If you're a handyman, maybe you wouldn't walk away when you realize the property will need a lot of repairs to be make-ready. Instead, you offer $164,000, get the property at a 20 percent discount, do a lot of the repairs yourself at minimal cost, and cash flow in year one.

3. Add value and increase your rent

This is the most risky of the three numbers to play with, but similar to the scenario we presented during the purchase price adjustment, if you have the expertise or extra room in your make-ready budget to add some extra touches to your property—add value—you can ask for prime rental rates. Again, this is very dependent on marketplace, location, and individual property, and you should be wary adjusting these numbers too much.

The more you analyze properties, the better you'll get at meeting and exceeding your financial goals. You may even want to up the ante in your goals, asking for a total ROI of 22 percent on an investment. Just know that this knack takes time and an incredible amount of analysis. Have fun playing with the numbers and learning the shortcuts, but don't rely on them—even as an advanced investor.

LEARN ANALYSIS SHORTCUTS

Though we've only walked through two hypothetical prospects, we recommend you work the worksheet numbers for many possible investments.

The more you use the analysis worksheet, the easier it will become to spot deals that fit your criteria. And, eventually, you'll hear experts using language and doing quick analyses based on some fast math rules of thumb. Just know that the experts always do their long math to make sure the short cut's outcome is on the mark. Three such methods used are as follows:

1. Capitalization Rate
2. Rent-to-Value Ratio
3. Cash-on-Cash Return

1. Capitalization Rate ("cap rate")

This rule of thumb is used to compare properties with different valuations. It helps investors quickly guesstimate a property's value based on the income it generates. The cap rate is computed by taking the net operating income and dividing it by the property's fair market value.

Net Operating Income / Fair Market Value = Cap Rate

For example, the cap rate for the single-family on Evergreen Terrace ($8,844/$150,000) is about 5.9 percent, whereas the cap rate for the duplex on Elm ($12,845/$205,000) is about 6.3 percent.

If you aren't willing to buy anything with a cap rate under 8 percent, both of these properties are immediately off the table, and you've saved yourself a lot of time completing full analysis on investments that fall outside your criteria. However, it's important to note that the cap rate is a rule of thumb that tells you a rate of return assuming that the property has no loan. Your actual rate of return will be affected by the financing you use.

You can use your cap rate for quick analysis in other ways as well. First, it's important to understand that the higher the cap rate, the better. For example, if you put your money in a savings account at 3 percent interest, your cap rate for that year is 3 percent. Since real estate can carry greater risk than other forms of investment, you should also expect higher cap rates.

For this reason, cap rates are a great way to compare property valuations. Let's step outside our Springfield properties for a moment and assume that you're looking at investing in two new properties. The first property has a projected NOI of $20,000 and an asking price of $500,000. The second property has a NOI of only $10,000, but an asking price of $110,000. Based on your cap rate calculations, the second property is the better investment, having a cap rate of 9 percent ($10,000 / $110,000) vs. a cap rate of 4 percent ($20,000 / $500,000).

2. Rent-to-Value Ratio

Another way to analyze a potential investment is to look at its current net rental income against its fair market value. This is called the rent-to-value ratio, and it's one of the most important concepts to understand as an investor because it can mean the difference between having cash flow and not. Here's a formula with our two example properties.

Gross Monthly Rental Income / Fair Market Value = Rent-to-Value Ratio

742 Evergreen Terrace Example: $1,390 / $150,000 = 0.93%

127 Elm Street Example: $1,975 / $205,000 = 0.96%

Some investors suggest that as long as you have a 1 percent rent-to-value ratio, you're going to have a positive cash flow—unless your expenses are exorbitantly high. Anything above that amount is gold. Both of our example properties fall short of this rule of thumb, so please understand the 1 percent rent-to-value ratio may not be achievable in many markets. But most markets have a magic number that represents value to experienced investors. Find out what that number is for you in your market.

3. Cash-on-Cash Return

This is another common rule of thumb that's used to calculate the return on your initial cash investment (down payment and any cost of repair) in year one. To compute the cash-on-cash return, you'll need your year-one cash flow numbers and your down payment numbers. Some investors also like to include the year-one make-ready repairs costs in their calculations, so we've shown both ways below:

Cash on Cash <u>without</u> Make-Ready Costs

Cash Flow / Initial Investment = (Year One) Cash-on-Cash Return

742 Evergreen Terrace Example: $809.47 / $33,750 = 2.3%

127 Elm Street Example: $1,864.70 / $46,125 = 4.0%

This shows how much out-of-pocket cash is returned to you each year. So, if you chose to buy the single-family property at 742 Evergreen Terrace, you would make a cash return of 2.3 percent on the $33,750 you paid for a down payment. Likewise, for 127 Elm Street, you would make a 4.0 percent cash return in year one. However, if you were to add your

$11,000 make-ready cash to the initial down payment, it would look something like this:

Cash on Cash <u>with</u> Make-Ready Costs

Cash Flow / Initial Investment = (Year One) Cash-on-Cash Return

742 Evergreen Terrace Example: $809.47 / $44,750 = 1.8%

127 Elm Street Example: $1,864.64 / $57,125 = 3.3%

Either way you decide to go—include the make-ready costs or not—the trick is to decide on a target cash-on-cash valuation before making a purchase decision. Then you can use the cash-on-cash method to help you quickly weed out prospective properties. Many real estate investors are happy to get a cash-on-cash return of 10 percent.

POINTS TO REMEMBER

Now that you have your analysis strategy in place and the tools to help you implement it, spotting those deals will become easier and easier. Just remember to continue dotting your "i's" and crossing your "t's." If you do your due diligence on the front end, your chances of finding great investments will skyrocket, and you'll be ready to make a purchase offer, as we'll do in "Buy" for both Springfield properties.

Keep in mind some core takeaways as you come to your purchase decision.

- **Don't overpay for a property.** You have predetermined financial criteria. Use the HOLD worksheet to analyze every prospect. Walk away from anything that doesn't fit your mold when it comes to numbers.

- **Stay in your chosen area.** You took time and energy during the Find process to arrive at a target location. Now stay on top of it. Continue to drive through and familiarize yourself with the neighborhood. This way you can keep an eye on your prospects and other comps in the area. Knowing your market like the back of your hand will only help you during the Buy, Manage, and Grow strategies.

- **Know going in.** Making sure you are clear on your musts and your wants prior to the analysis is key. Not only can you then start to use quick calculations preanalysis, you won't be deterred by your emotions.

STAGE 3: BUY

✓
1. FIND
The right property for the right terms and the right price

Outcome: a list of qualified investment properties from which to choose

↓

✓
2. ANALYZE
A property to make sure the numbers and the terms make sense

Outcome: a prospect that meets your financial criteria

↓

3. BUY
An investment property where you make money going in

☐ **Chapter 9**: Arrange Financing

☐ **Chapter 10**: Write and Present the Offer

☐ **Chapter 11**: Close the Purchase

↓

Outcome: a profitable property to add to your HOLD investment portfolio

Start out with an ideal and end up with a deal.

KARL ALBRECHT

You have put in hours of planning and research. You've purposefully traveled neighborhoods in search of your ideal location. You've met with real estate agents, contractors, and prospective sellers. And after analyzing your two Springfield properties against others and from every angle, you're ready to purchase a long-term investment property! And, as luck would have it, you've got two options that you're going to continue pursuing—one single-family home and one duplex.

Buying either option will be one of the most critical parts of your journey because this is where you turn from a "would-be" to a "for-real" HOLD investor. This is where you make the offer, do your final due diligence, write the down payment check, and take possession of *your* investment property. It's no wonder this is also where excitement and, at times, anxiety can run high ... Don't fret! This is normal.

Just remember, you've already analyzed your single-family home—against several others—so you know if you buy it *right*, you will be making your money going in, which will minimize your risk. You're not interested in 742 Evergreen Terrace and 127 Elm Street because they *may become* good deals. You know they *are already* good deals. They meet your personal and property criteria and cash flow in year one—and, if they appreciate, that's just icing on the cake. If you've come this far with a property, the buying part should be the natural next step.

While we can't completely eliminate the inevitable angst that accompanies any purchase of this size—real estate or otherwise—we can guide you through the ins and outs of the Buy phase. We're here to help you make wise choices, to put your feet firmly on the road to successful long-term real estate investing, and to point out any potential pitfalls to your successes.

In this section, we'll discuss what the Buy process looks like—how to arrange financing and the various strategies, how to write and present an offer, and finally, we'll guide you through the closing process, from inspections to signing the closing documents.

Before we dive in, it's important to note that your investment team will be in close contact during this period of the HOLD strategy. Take advantage of those strong relationships you've worked so hard to build—your agent, lender, title company, contractor, property manager, attorney, etc. Think of them as your network of experts there to answer questions, provide guidance, and offer solutions. They are truly the ones who will make the process run smoothly, and they'll share in your triumph!

CHAPTER 9: ARRANGE FINANCING

✓	**1. FIND** The right property for the right terms and the right price

Outcome: a list of qualified investment properties from which to choose

↓

✓	**2. ANALYZE** A property to make sure the numbers and the terms make sense

Outcome: a prospect that meets your financial criteria

↓

3. BUY
An investment property where you make money going in

☐ **Chapter 9**: Arrange Financing

☐ **Chapter 10**: Write and Present the Offer

☐ **Chapter 11**: Close the Purchase

↓

Outcome: a profitable property to add to your HOLD investment portfolio

After reading this chapter, you will know how to:

☐ Understand the basics of conventional lending strategies.

☐ Find and attract private lending sources.

☐ Use unconventional options for backup financing solutions.

UNDERSTAND CONVENTIONAL LENDING

Financing is the tool you use to accomplish your goals and a key part of your HOLD strategy. The right financing package can have a positive effect on your profits—either by accelerating your equity or increasing your cash flow. Getting your financing in order is also a prerequisite for making an offer. Before a seller will take a property off the market, they need to know that you can actually complete the purchase. This is where the prequalification process discussed in chapter 2 of the Find section comes into play. Most sellers will look for you to at least be prequalified, but more likely preapproved to even consider accepting your offer.

Think about it. This makes perfect sense. From the time a seller accepts an offer to the final closing date can take between 30 and 45 days. And, as you know, time is money. During this period, they may have to make an extra mortgage payment and their move may be delayed. And, if something falls through and they have to put the property back on the market, other buyers may assume the property has issues that they'll want to avoid and steer clear.

Obtaining the preapproval letter from your lender is at least a way for the seller to know that you are financially capable of closing the deal. That being said, the first rule of financing real estate is that there is no cookie-cutter formula. Each deal must stand on its own merit as to whether it works or doesn't work for you. Mortgage financing is ever changing. Markets heat up and cool down. Interest rates rise and fall. Yesterday's flow of free and easy money dries up overnight.

Regardless of the state of the market or your income, asset, or credit situation, there will always be opportunities and ways for you to capitalize on them. In this chapter, we will discuss three types of financing strategies:

1. Conventional Loans

2. Private Lending

3. Creative Financing

Each will have its own advantages and drawbacks, and we will help you find a financing solution that's right for you.

1. Conventional Loans

The most popular loans are conventional or conforming loans, which are fixed-rate mortgages typically financed for 30 years. They can also be packaged in five-year increments ranging from 10 to 40 years.

Simply put, a conventional loan is a lending agreement that is not guaranteed or insured by the federal government. For this reason, conventional loans do not follow the same strict guidelines as loans that are guaranteed by the government under the Federal Housing Administration (FHA) or Veterans Affairs (VA). Conventional loans come in two types: conforming or nonconforming.

Conforming vs. nonconforming

Conforming loans have terms and conditions that follow the guidelines set forth by Fannie Mae and Freddie Mac, the government-sponsored corporations that were created to purchase mortgage loans, package them into securities, and sell the securities to investors in order to keep a flow of money available for home buyers. Their prevalence often translates to more competitive rates. On the other hand, nonconforming loans are loans that are not eligible for sale to either Fannie Mae or Freddie Mac for various reasons, including loan amount, characteristics, or underwriting guidelines. For example, a jumbo loan is a loan that exceeds the current conforming loan limit. Say the limit is $417,000 and you want to buy a $600,000 property with 25 percent down, your loan would exceed the conforming limit, and you'd want to speak with your lender about options.

However, nine times out of ten, investors will use conforming loans to purchase a property or they'll bring cash to the table. Again, we suggest discussing all financing with your HOLD investment team—specifically your agent and lender—to decide what combination works best for you.

Building your mortgage team

There are basically two sources for conventional lending: mortgage bankers who work for retail banks and typically lend their own money, and mortgage brokers who find money from various sources for you. Each one has advantages. Mortgage bankers approve loans directly and generally have greater leeway to make a lending decision. Mortgage brokers can search through the landscape of lenders to find a rate and mortgage program that best fits your requirements.

According to mortgage broker David Reed, author of numerous books and articles on financing real estate, the key to successful borrowing is to find the best lender and within that organization find the most experienced loan officer and stick with her. An experienced loan officer knows how to put a deal together, can counsel you on the best financing package, and will alert you to the advantages and pitfalls.

"The top agents who do hundreds of deals will know who the top loan officers are in your area," Reed says. "It takes a long time for a loan officer to get on a top agent's short list. They need at least ten years of experience, preferably in preautomated underwriting, and a track record of being able to close a deal fast, give solid advice, and quote accurate rates within a 0.25 percent variance."

That's not all. Experienced loan officers are an investor's best friend. They will not only assist you with your immediate investment financing needs, they'll alert you when it's the best time to refinance or if a new and advantageous loan program becomes available.

"You're investing in real estate," says Reed, "not in keeping up with the day-to-day mortgage rates. A trusted loan officer can do all that for you."

Meeting conventional loan criteria

In a traditional scenario, a buyer financing with a conventional loan will put 20 percent down and finance 80 percent. Buyers that do not have the 20 percent down payment can still qualify for a loan but would be required to pay private mortgage insurance or PMI, which protects the lender in the event the buyer defaults on their loan. That being said, many lenders expect investors to put down 25 percent, since they will not be occupying the residence and are therefore, more of a risk. To reinforce this norm, we analyzed the Springfield properties at 25 percent. Obviously you'll want to reanalyze the numbers at 20 percent if your lender permits you to go with the traditional 20/80 split. Not having to pony up that extra 5 percent is a huge bonus but is not always possible.

Simply having the right amount of cash on hand for the down payment does not make you a qualified investor. You'll also need to meet certain income and credit criteria to be eligible for financing. As we discussed in chapter 2 of "Find," this is generally a two-step process. First, you will need to be prequalified by your lender by documenting your financial background—credit history, employment history, education, and any accounts or assets. Step two will be a more thorough verification process where you'll be asked to provide recent pay stubs, bank and credit statements, etc., for every item listed in your prequalification phase. At the end of the process, your lender will approve you for the loan and provide you with a good faith estimate and an official letter of preapproval. She will also disclose interest rates, estimated taxes and insurance, the monthly mortgage payment, and any other loan-related expenses. You will present this document to the seller with your offer. Again, since loan requirements are much more stringent for investors, your rates may tend to be a bit higher than a home buyer's.

Some additional investor guidelines to note are the number of properties you own, your previous landlord experience, and your cash reserves.

I. **Number of properties owned** – There are a finite number of homes that you as an investor can finance conventionally. The number depends on the financial market and on conventional lenders' levels of risk aversion. There have been times when investors could finance as many as 12 homes conventionally, and other times when it was as few as 4. This doesn't mean that if you own more properties than current Fannie Mae and Freddie Mac restrictions allow you won't be able to obtain financing. The limitation is on the number of properties that *currently* have mortgages on them. Jim and Linda once put a contract on a house before they realized three-quarters of the way through the process that they had too many conforming loans to qualify for conventional financing. Luckily, they were able to go to the bank and arrange for another source of financing—discussion to follow—or else they would have missed the opportunity to buy a great investment property.

II. **Previous landlord experience** – If you are using the rental income from the property to qualify for the mortgage, lenders usually require you to have two years of rental management experience. The requirement may be waived if you have sufficient cash reserves that meet standard guidelines.

III. **Cash reserves** – The reserves calculation is based on the monthly housing expense of the financed property, including homeowner association dues, cooperative fees, and other loans secured by the property, along with the mortgage, taxes, and insurance. You may need to have several months' worth of cash reserves on the financed property, plus three to six months additional reserve. So let's say you want to finance an investment property costing $100,000, resulting in total monthly payments of $1,000. Here's how the numbers might look:

25% down payment	$25,000
Six months reserve	$6,000
Closing costs (estimated)	$5,000
Total cash required	**$36,000**

The total cash reserves required by conventional lenders can vary greatly depending on the overall lending climate. When lenders are skittish, they require more for less. Other times, your loan officer can get you up to speed on the current norms with a quick conversation.

Consider owner-occupied financing

Invariably, whenever we teach a real estate class, someone will ask what to do if they aren't able to meet the conventional lending requirements for investors. A classic option is owner-occupied financing. Basically, you buy a property, live there for set amount of time—typically one to two years—and then trade up and keep it as an investment. As long as you meet the minimum credit score, you can usually purchase an investment with less up front and lower rates by avoiding the hefty cash reserve requirement, bringing less cash to the table and locking in better interest rates.

To qualify for owner-occupied financing, you will likely have to sign a document at closing that identifies the property as your personal residence and that you intend to live there. It is fraud to claim you're living there or intend to live there for that time allotment if you don't actually do so, but once the occupancy requirement is met, the terms of the loan contract remain in effect for as long as you own that property. That is, however, provided you make your monthly loan payments, properly insure and maintain the property, and pay your taxes on time.

After you have lived in the house for the required term of occupancy, you can buy another property at a favorable owner-occupied loan rate, move into it, and find a good tenant to rent the first home. We've seen a number of examples where people would refinance their home, pull cash out if they had ample equity, and use it to buy another home to live in. With this strategy, they acquired several rental properties and their primary residence with favorable terms and relatively low down payments.

To summarize, the advantages of owner-occupied financing are:

I.   A better interest rate

II. Lower down payment

III. Less cash reserve required

IV. Better terms than nonowner-occupied financing

The bottom line: To obtain a conventional loan, you will need to have cash, experience, good credit, or seek another source of financing. Of course, as we stated at the start of this chapter, the rules of financing are always changing according to the conditions of the market, the broader economy, as well as governmental action. So stay in close connection with your mortgage team.

2. Private Lending

Whether you have lots of money and great credit or no money and problematic credit, there may be times when you need investor partners and private lenders to help fund your real estate venture. Private lending means that the loan is not going to be sold to Fannie Mae or Freddie Mac. It is important to note that regulations on private lending vary from state-to-state and even on a local level. Make sure to get educated on your specific location prior to going this route. Our aim is to give you an overview and some options in this branch of financing. If you're seriously considering private lending, you'll need to call in your real estate attorney. A specialist can not only educate you on the process, they can provide invaluable counsel on avoiding the many pitfalls of private lending.

Private money can come from anywhere. It could come from someone's retirement account, syndicates, from an individual who has cash and wants a stable return, or from the most common form of private residential lending: owner financing. Because the loan is not going to be sold on the secondary market, there are no set guidelines for terms. You can work out whatever terms are found to be mutually beneficial for both you and the lender as long as your respective attorney signs off on them.

When Jim and Linda's nephew Randy Barber moved to Denton, Texas, to go to college, he rented a house from them and also managed the three houses on the property. Randy soon decided that he wanted to be the guy with the properties collecting his own rent. Today, he owns 26 rental units that cash flow $5,500 a month.

Randy uses a combination of bank financing and private money. One of his first investors was his mother. She had inherited money from her mother and put it into a CD. Randy borrowed money against the CD to buy and flip two properties. He paid her back and gave her a $10,000 return on her investment. He's in another partnership now with a friend from school. Randy finds the property and handles all the details of buying and flipping, while his friend puts up the money in exchange for 40 percent of the profits. Recently, they were contacted by a woman whose home was in foreclosure. They paid her note and, in exchange, she deeded them the property. Randy fixed up the house, arranged the sale, and divided the profits between the partnership and the homeowner—a win-win for all parties.

Pros and Cons of Private Lending

I. Investor and Syndicates

Pros 1. Less out-of-pocket money

2. Increased buying power that can lead to affording great deals

Cons 1. Financial ties with a second (or third) party

2. All involved parties need to be on the same page up front—needs to run like a business

II. Owner Financing

Pros 1. Avoid conventional requirements

2. Potentially no points or closing costs

3. More aspects of the sale open to negotiation

Cons 1. Overall property cost may be higher

2. May be charged a higher interest rate

III. Local Banks

Pros 1. Increased processing and closing

2. Getting a loan that wouldn't necessarily be approved under conventional guidelines

Cons 1. Possibility of higher interest rates

2. A larger down payment

3. Shorter maturity time

IV. Partnerships

Pros 1. Can reduce your risk

2. Can make up for what you're lacking—larger down payment, strong financial statements, etc.

3. Partners may have experience, time, or expertise to lend outside of finances

Cons 1. Since you share in the cost, you also must share the success

2. Can lose control of the business based on decision-making strategies

3. Partner may buy you out

Figure 9-1

Lack of money can seem like an insurmountable obstacle to overcome. But it can be addressed if, like Randy and other investors we know, you apply determination, creativity, and some well-known financing strategies. Some opportunities to consider are investors and syndicates, owner financing, local banks, and partnerships. Figure 9-1 gives the comparative nutshell version of the pros and cons of these four options, but we'll discuss each more in depth.

I. Investors and syndicates

A time-honored solution for finding investment capital is the "angel" investor. Finding investors is really a matter of networking. Talk to your banker, who may want to offer you a loan and may also know interested investors. Try the chamber of commerce and any other business organizations you belong to. Companies that manage self-directed IRA accounts may have people looking to lend. Go to your local real estate associations. Let people know you're looking for money investors, and that you are in search of investor partners for real estate investing. Find out who has been successful and how many deals they've done.

If you know someone with money—maybe a family member or a friend—approach and educate them. Friends and family are some of the most dependable resources for any entrepreneur. For instance, Steve's first investor was his grandfather. In the late 1970s, when interest rates hovered close to 20 percent, his grandfather was making 9 percent interest on his CDs. Steve matched the CD rate, promised his grandfather 10 percent of the profits, and started his investing career. One of his clients, a twenty-six-year-old firefighter, is now using a similar approach with his grandfather.

Just be sure that before you start looking for that angel, you pull together a business plan. Everyone, maybe even your grandfather, is going to want a solid five-year business plan complete with financial projections. This kind of financing is sometimes called "hard money" for a reason. These investors are sharing more of the risk than traditional lenders, and, in return, will likely have touch criteria and terms you must meet to avoid default.

Another approach is to put together an investment syndicate to pool money and buy multiple properties. It could be a group of friends or people you meet at an investment club. During a real estate downturn, four young Phoenix firefighters in their twenties and thirties formed a syndicate with money they borrowed from their friends and family. Their goal was to buy and flip properties in order to pay off their investors and ultimately raise the capital to purchase and hold income-producing properties. As a result, they were able to significantly increase their buying power and take advantage of a historic buyer's market.

Figure 9-2 shares some tips for forming an investment syndicate.

Tips to Form an Investment Syndicate

1. Choose people you get along with. Find people with similar investing styles and goals. If there's bad chemistry, you're setting yourself up for personal and legal problems.

2. Keep it small. You need enough people to have an adequate amount of money, but not so many that it complicates decision-making.

3. Run it like a business. The firefighters created an LLC with clearly stated rules about who holds the money, how it will be used, and who makes decisions.

4. Follow the rules. You can never be too careful when managing yours and other people's money in a committee or group setting.

Figure 9-2

Owner financing is when the seller of a property acts as a bank and loans the purchaser all or part of the money needed to purchase the property. There are a number of advantages to the seller for carrying a note. If the owner is having trouble selling the property, owner financing can be an inducement to prospective buyers. There may be tax advantages to the seller in spreading out over time when the owner receives money from the sale of a property. And many owners simply like the idea that they can receive a monthly income from a property even after they have sold it.

We know of an elderly widow who moved into a retirement home when she could no longer maintain her house. Rather than selling her house outright, she opted to owner-finance it and used the income for her retirement.

What's more, the owner can charge the buyer interest on the money. That way he not only collects a monthly mortgage payment on the property, but the interest as well, effectively increasing the overall sale proceeds of the property. Many people have built financial wealth by owning a large portfolio of properties, getting them paid off, and then selling them through owner financing.

Here's how it works. Let's say an elderly couple owned their house free and clear and lived in it for 30 years. The couple is currently earning about 3 percent on their CDs and looking for an investment that provides a better rate of return. The house is worth $150,000. They decide to sell you their house with a very low down payment and finance it for you at 8 percent interest over 15 years, or 10 years. They're getting a first lien position on the house, so if you default on the loan, they get the house back and can sell it again. The advantage for the owners is that they're usually getting a higher rate of interest—a point or two above the going rate—because the transaction is considered higher risk.

Oftentimes an owner may offer owner financing if the property has been on the market awhile or it needs work. Such cases may provide an opportunity for a buyer to negotiate below-market terms or price.

Another option is to have the seller carry a second mortgage behind the first lien from the mortgage company. For example, let's say you find a duplex selling for $250,000 and don't have the 25 percent down payment that a traditional lender requires. With owner financing, you can put down 15 percent, the seller finances another 10 percent, and the mortgage company finances the loan at 75 percent of the purchase price. You put less money down and also avoid having to pay property mortgage insurance (PMI). Just ensure you disclose everything in writing with your mortgage lender. Disclose, disclose, disclose! At different times, mortgage lenders have been very open to these creative arrangements, but they have to know about them. Full disclosure is always the smart choice.

III. Local banks

For many investors, their community bank may be their best friend. Most banks have a certain number of loans they keep in house instead of selling them to Fannie Mae or Freddie Mac on the secondary market. The term for this is "portfolio lending" because they keep the loan in house, or in their portfolio.

Portfolio lenders tend to be smaller community banks—often privately held or credit unions—that have more flexibility in the loan-granting process than larger, publicly traded institutions. With a portfolio loan, you may have more flexible guidelines for the number of properties owned or previous property management experience, or you use the rental income to qualify. Just like the bankers of old, they can assess your overall situation, look at the intangibles as well as the tangibles of a transaction, and even ask for and evaluate business references. A long-term banking relationship might result in a positive loan decision, even in a case where there has been a period of poor credit.

Portfolio lenders can't be reckless in their lending practices or they will quickly go out of business. But they can go beyond lending guidelines as long as they have a good reason. A local bank is often more interested in loaning to its immediate community, seeing it as an investment in their customers, creating growth, and contributing to a healthy business environment.

When Jim and Linda were just getting started, they walked into their local bank with a business plan and a strategy to purchase two properties before the end of the year. The banker committed to lending them 80 percent of the appraised value of the property and to close on the properties within two weeks of making the deal.

Jim credits this to the fact that small banks are usually relationship based. The key is to network and get into a relationship with the decision makers. "Our reputation in real estate was well known in the market. In bigger banks where people may come and go quickly, they may not know about my reputation in real estate," Jim says. "They may be looking at you as a number, a credit score, and not what your past or future is. You need a relationship with a decision maker: someone who knows you, understands who you are, has faith in you, and is willing to take on your loan and your risk."

All banks are not the same—many have a particular niche they're trying to fill in the marketplace. Some banks specialize in lending to businesses; others like commercial real estate deals; some specialize in construction loans. It's important to understand what a bank likes to do. Through networking you can find out which banks are good at doing real estate investment lending.

IV. Partnerships

Real estate partnerships have been around since the beginning of real estate investing for a simple reason: creating the $1 + 1 = 3$ effect. In the words of Solomon: "Two can accomplish more than twice as much as one. If one fails, the other pulls him up; but if a man falls when he is alone, he's in trouble. And one standing alone can be attacked and defeated, but two can stand back-to-back and conquer."

Jennice and Steve have successfully partnered on a number of real estate investments over the years. As a real estate investor, a partnership can reduce your risk and increase your leverage. It provides you with what you may lack—be it a larger down payment, stronger financial statements, or greater experience. On the other hand, partnerships come with their fair share of disadvantages. You are expected to share the rewards if the business is successful. You could lose total control over the business if you and your partner have difficulty in making decisions or if your partner's judgment is poor. And if a conflict arises, one partner may end up buying out the other one.

Jim and Linda purchased their first property in partnership with a builder. They found the property, a fixer-upper located in a desirable area, well below market price. Knowing a good deal when they saw it but lacking the money to make it happen, they partnered with a builder they knew who was able to borrow money for the purchase and make the repairs. Another partner was someone they knew from the restaurant business. Everyone pooled their resources, formed a company, and ended up buying more than 100 properties together. That partnership has lasted for decades.

With the experience of this partnership and several others, Jim and Linda advise that bad partnerships can be worse than your worst dating nightmare. "If it weren't for partnering with the right people, we wouldn't be here today. We started out without any cash and had to figure out how to leverage ourselves into the game." Partnerships are another form of leverage— leveraging money, people, and relationships in order to get what you want as long as you have the right safeguards.

To help you evaluate and find the right partnerships, we put together some do's and do not's, seen in figure 9-3.

The Do's and Do Not's of Partnerships

Do ...

- [ ] Find out about your prospective partners, and be comfortable with their reputations and capabilities.

- [ ] Write a business plan that includes goals, priorities, and strategies to make sure both partners have the same vision, ideas, and direction.

- [ ] Start with an operating agreement that outlines each partner's responsibilities, the goals of the partnership, and builds in as many contingencies as possible.

- [ ] Start with a small deal as a test run. If it makes money and everyone does what's expected, take it to the next level. In other words, date first and see if you get along before you marry.

(continued)

Do Not ...

- ☐ Over-commit and under-deliver. That only damages trust.
- ☐ Do it just for the money. Do it because you have a common vision. A partnership can't work if you and your partner's visions aren't aligned.
- ☐ Move forward until everything is in writing. Small disagreements can lead to big problems.

Figure 9-3

The overarching theme is make sure everyone involved is on the same page. Do not go into a partnership blindly, and be very clear about expectations, rules, and goals. As part of this, you'll want to draw up a partnership agreement. Figure 9-4 is an example of things to include in your agreement, but we suggest verifying your document with all partners and respective attorneys.

Partnership Agreement Checklist

- ☐ Reason for forming the company and goals the company wants to achieve
- ☐ How and when proceeds should be allocated
- ☐ Capital investment (initial contributions)
- ☐ Value of the investments
- ☐ Management strategy for the partnership
- ☐ How and when to make partnership decisions
- ☐ How and when to make the decision to sell an investment or buy more
- ☐ How to allocate profits and/or losses
- ☐ How to liquidate distributions if and when the company is dissolved
- ☐ What to do in the event of the death or incompetence of a partner
- ☐ Life insurance to buy out the other person's family
- ☐ Buy-sell agreement with right of first refusal
- ☐ How to handle dispute resolution so that you avoid ending up in court

Figure 9-4

3. Creative Financing

Unconventional lending, also known as creative financing, is just what it sounds like: nontraditional means of financing, or financing techniques not commonly used. Creative financing doesn't mean tricky or fraudulent. It simply takes legitimate lending rules and applies them in a different way. That being said, it is important to enter into creative financing with a deep understanding of terms and possible outcomes, as it can be riskier than conventional financing.

The reasons an investor will enter into an unconventional loan agreement could be credit issues, or simply because they don't meet one or more of the traditional lending requirements for investors. For instance, they may not have a sufficient down payment or they don't have enough property management experience.

One of the benefits of unconventional financing is that, if done correctly, you may be able to purchase or finance a property by leveraging other people's money (OPM) and using as little of your own money as possible. A few examples are wraparound loans, lease options, and lease purchases. As with private lending, before heading down any of these paths, consult with your attorney and research the process thoroughly.

Wraparound loans

Wraparound loans or "wraps" are a type of seller financing in which the seller extends to the buyer a secondary mortgage, which "wraps around" any existing mortgages already secured by the property. Wraps are oftentimes seen as a dirty word in the investment business, but they do exist and many expert investors still use them often. At different times in history, wraps have been very common, but they have also been abused. Some investors entered into wraps without their lender's consent and, as a result, most mortgage loans include a "due on sale" clause that legally restricts a wrap without the lender's approval. Our suggestion: If you are interested in using a wrap, proceed with caution and fully disclose the wrap up front with your lender.

To better exemplify what a wrap is, let's say Joe has a $75,000 mortgage on his home. He sells his home to Janis for $100,000. She pays him $5,000 down and executes a promissory note for $95,000 to pay him for the balance of the sale price. Joe's existing mortgage stays in place and the balance of his equity—$20,000—is received in monthly payments. Janis makes payments including interest on her loan each month to Joe, who is then responsible for making payments to the original lender. Should she default on those payments, Joe has the right to foreclose and reclaim his property.

Because wraps are a form of seller financing, a buyer can purchase property without having to qualify for a loan. They can also expedite the process of purchasing a home.

Wraps are attractive to sellers, because they can leverage a lower interest rate on the existing mortgage into a higher yield for themselves. Returning to our example, suppose Joe's $75,000 mortgage has a rate of 6 percent and Janis' new mortgage for $95,000 has a rate of 8 percent. Not only does Joe earn 8 percent on his $20,000, he also earns the 2 percent difference on $70,000.

There's one more benefit for Joe. His payment on the $75,000 is $650 a month. Janis' is $900. Therefore, Joe is receiving $250 a month in cash flow, and Janis is paying the taxes, insurance payment, and maintenance.

Sound good? It is important to note, however, that there are downsides to wraps for both the seller and buyer. In general, only assumable loans, or loans in which existing borrowers can transfer their obligations to qualified house purchasers, are "wrappable." Today, most fixed-rate loans carry "due on sale" clauses, which require that the mortgage be repaid in full if the property is sold. Due on sale prohibits a home purchaser from assuming a seller's existing mortgage without the lender's permission. If permission is given, it will always be at the current market rate. Without that permission, there is a possibility that the originating lender may discover the transaction and call the loan due.

Again, if you are contemplating a wrap, take caution. You could be forced out of the property if the lender calls the loan due, and the secondary lender (seller) doesn't have the money to pay for it. In this case, you would have to refinance the loan at current interest rates and terms or risk losing the property in a foreclosure. Though not illegal, wraps give the lender the option to accelerate the loan. The buyer also runs the risk that the seller will pocket their payments and not pay the monthly note. While this is certainly a violation of the agreement, the buyer will still be in default. One way to prevent this scenario is through using a third-party collector or guarantor.

When we said proceed with caution, we meant it. Wraps are rare for a reason.

Jim has a successful wraparound loan on one of his properties, which he executed through the bank that holds the original mortgage. The buyer, a local contractor, was unable to qualify for a conventional loan, but Jim knew that he was hard working and a good credit risk. Jim sold him the house, wrapping the new loan into the existing one at an interest rate that was 1.5 percent higher than what he was paying. The bank agreed to the wrap with the understanding that Jim would continue to make payments on the original loan.

Lease options

A lease option, or a lease with an option to buy, is a simple way to control a property when you don't have the means (financial, credit, or criteria) to secure a conventional loan to purchase it.

In a lease option, the tenants/buyers sign a lease agreement for a set number of years with an option that gives them the exclusive right to purchase the home for a predetermined price at the end of the agreement. If the tenant does not exercise his right to purchase the property, the owner can sell the property to someone else.

This type of arrangement can be advantageous for a seller because he will likely get cash on the front end to secure the lease option, a long-term lease, and a tenant who takes care of the property as if he owned it. If the tenant purchases the property at the end of the lease-option period, the owner gets the contractual price and any cash flow from the previous monthly payments.

For an investor, a lease option enables you to control a property worth much more than what you could normally afford to purchase for one to five years, depending on the terms. As long as the agreement gives you the right to sublease the property, you can rent it, choose the tenants, and collect any amount above your monthly rent as cash flow. Make sure your agreement specifically allows you to sublet the property. If you do go with a lease option and the property increases in value, you can sell it at the end of the option period and make a profit.

One investor we know, for instance, has more than 20 properties with mortgages—more than the number allowed for a conventional mortgage. He uses lease options to control a property for a period of time. Then he puts a tenant in to cover the option and provide cash flow. At the end of the term, he will exercise his option to purchase the property and then either hold it or, if the property has appreciated sufficiently, sell it to capture the spread.

Similarly, there are investors who have used lease options as the basis for a very successful HOLD strategy. One of them is Michigan real estate agent and author of several how-to books on creative financing, Wendy Patton. She has executed more than 600 transactions since her first real estate investment in the mid-'80s. "It's a great strategy for someone who wants to HOLD the properties long term," Wendy says. "You can buy a property on a long-term option, rent it, and take the cash flow—especially if you have an agreement where you're building a lot of equity."

For instance, eight years ago she bought an option on a property from a seller who retired and moved away. Wendy executed an option for $900 a month, $500 of which went toward the purchase price. She is not allowed to buy the property until after his death because he doesn't want to pay capital gains taxes on a property that he owns free and clear. Under the terms of their agreement, he gets $900 a month cash flow, but he only has to pay taxes on the $400 portion because the option credit isn't taxable until she exercises the option or forfeits and walks away.

"With a lease option there are some really creative things you can do, depending on the seller's situation. The key is to negotiate an arrangement that's a win for the seller and a win for you."

1. **Price** - How much money is needed to secure the property, and what's the final purchase price?

2. **Monthly Payments** - What is the monthly cost of the lease option and, of that, how much gets applied to the purchase price?

3. **Length of Time** - Timing is always negotiable. What's the length of the term?

Figure 9-5

Lease purchases

"Lease purchase" is a term often used interchangeably with "lease option," but there are some significant differences. A lease option is, in effect, the purchase of time. The tenant/buyer purchases the exclusive right to purchase property for a predetermined price within a specified period of time, but he or she has no vested interest in the property.

In a lease purchase, you are contractually *obligated* to purchase the property at the end of the lease-purchase term. The owner agrees to sell the property to the lessee at a specific price on a specific future date and typically charges higher than the fair market rent. The difference is applied toward the potential down payment.

With a lease purchase, you have two binding contracts: the lease contract and the purchase contract. The lease purchase outlines all the terms of the deal, just like a regular purchase contract, including a specific close of escrow date.

Similar to an installment loan for an automobile, the owner holds legal title to the property as security for payment, while the buyer has "equitable" title. Meanwhile, the buyer has the right to live in the property, rent it, and otherwise enjoy all of the benefits of ownership.

For example, let's say you bought a house for $220,000 through a lease purchase and five years from now the property appraises for $275,000. With appreciation you now have $55,000 in equity in the property. When you go to buy the home, you've already got a 20 percent down payment, which means that you won't have to purchase private mortgage insurance.

Even if the property does not appreciate to the extent that you expect, as a smart investor you've structured a deal with low monthly payments, or with significant option credits from each month's rental payments. Option credits are the amounts applied out of the monthly rent during the option period and credited against the purchase price of the property when you buy it. The amount of option credits is negotiable and, again, should be included as a clause in your lease purchase contract. Wendy Patton has negotiated as much as 100 percent of the rent to be applied as option credits! Although that's far from typical, it's not a bad idea to ask for more than you want in order to settle on a number that is close to what you actually want.

Still, you should proceed cautiously with a lease purchase because it *obligates* you to buy the property even if the market sours and the property is worth less than the locked-in price. If you stick with properties where the market is appreciating rapidly, or you've struck a deal that's a great investment no matter what, a lease purchase can be a lucrative investment strategy.

Both lease options and lease purchases are ways to acquire investment property if you can't qualify for a conventional loan. The lease option is a landlord-tenant arrangement until the purchase is complete. The lease purchase is a sale at the inception of the agreement. So which formula is better? It depends on the situation and your goals. Figure 9-6 will help you determine which route might be better for you.

Lease Option vs. Lease Purchase

Lease Option

1. Get a long-term lease that gives you control of the property without a down payment.

2. You can buy the home at any time during the contract.

3. You are the only one with the option to buy the property during the lease period.

4. In an appreciating market, you may get a good deal if the home's value exceeds your locked-in purchase price.

5. You have a chance to clean up your credit and build equity.

6. You have the option not to purchase.

Lease Purchase

1. No down payment necessary.

2. Assuming the property meets your investment criteria, you'll have time to put together the money you need to purchase it.

3. You have the same tax benefits as if you held the legal title.

4. You can lock in at today's price and build equity if the market appreciates.

5. This shares the advantages of a wrap-around loan without triggering the "due on sale" clause in most states.

Figure 9-6

Regardless of which you choose, make sure and do your due diligence before you sign anything. Figure 9-7 will help you keep important tasks top of mind.

1. Do a home inspection. Be as detailed as possible—photograph and document the condition of the property and any necessary repairs.

2. Make sure all payments are current, such as mortgage, taxes, and insurance, and verify if there are any liens against the property.

3. Spell out the terms of the lease option. As an investor, you want to get as long term a lease option as possible.

4. Arrange to pay the mortgage company directly instead of paying the seller. If the mortage payment is higher than the rental payment, get proof the seller is paying the overage, and specify a penalty if they fail to do so.

5. Put eveything in writing—option contracts must include the same information you'd find in sales contracts in order to be enforceable.

6. Call on experts to assist you through the process. Make sure you understand the contract and complete a successful transaction.

Figure 9-7

FINANCE YOUR SPRINGFIELD PROPERTIES

Now that we've walked through various financing strategies, let's return to your Springfield properties—the single-family home at 742 Evergreen Terrace and the duplex at 127 Elm Street. To keep our HOLD strategy in line with the most common investment type, we've decided to finance with a conventional loan on a 30-year note. We are going to keep our interest rates the same as in "Analyze"—again working off a 30-year median—but this is where you would revisit your worksheet to lock in your current rates and reassess the numbers in preparation to make your offer.

- The right financing package can have a positive effect on your profits—either by accelerating your accumulation of equity or increasing your cash flow.

- There are three methods of financing your investment:

  1. *Conventional* or conforming loans, the most popular lending instruments, are fixed-rate mortgages typically financed for 30 years. Conventional loans have specific terms and conditions that follow the guidelines set forth by Fannie Mae and Freddie Mac and may not be the best route for an investor who lacks some of the requirements needed to secure the loan.

  2. *Private* loans are not sold to Freddie Mac or Fannie Mae and are not subject to the same guidelines as conventional loans. Private lending can come from family and friends, investors, partnerships, owner financing, the local bank, or any other private source.

  3. *Creative* financing takes the rules of funding and applies them in different ways, such as lease options, lease purchases, and wraparound loans. Although you will need to be aware of the risks, if done correctly, creative financing may enable you to purchase or finance a property by leveraging other people's money.

- Maintain an open mind. Remember that regardless of the state of the market or your income, asset, or credit situation, there will always be opportunities and ways for you to capitalize on them. If the right investment comes up, weigh your financing options before walking away.

CHAPTER 10:
WRITE AND PRESENT THE OFFER

✓	**1. FIND** **The right property for the right terms and the right price**

Outcome: a list of qualified investment properties from which to choose

↓

✓	**2. ANALYZE** **A property to make sure the numbers and the terms make sense**

Outcome: a prospect that meets your financial criteria

↓

3. BUY
An investment property where you make money going in

- ☑ **Chapter 9**: Arrange Financing
- ☐ **Chapter 10**: Write and Present the Offer
- ☐ **Chapter 11**: Close the Purchase

↓

Outcome: a profitable property to add to your HOLD investment portfolio

After reading this chapter, you will know how to:

- ☐ Structure the offer letter.

- ☐ Bulletproof the purchase contract.

- ☐ Negotiate a win-win transaction.

When it's time to make an offer on a property, there are two things you'll need to consider: price and terms. If you give up something on the price, you should always try to make it back with the terms. In a real estate deal, everything is negotiable—not only the price, but also the occupancy date, what personal property is included, who pays closing costs ... everything. Ask for what you want in your initial offer. You may not get it, but you should always ask.

Throughout the process, a good real estate agent will be invaluable in preparing, submitting, and negotiating the offer. Even though many investors have their real estate license, they still use another agent to help prepare, submit, and negotiate the offer. There's an old saying that a lawyer who represents himself has a fool for a client. The same thing applies to a real estate agent.

Your agent is one of the most important people on your HOLD team. Just as he has had the information on location, comps, rental comps, and other professionals to include in your team, he should also understand investment properties and your investment strategy. During the Buy process, your agent helps you evaluate what to offer based on your criteria and their own research and knowledge of the market. So, you need a responsive agent negotiator who can present the offer quickly since time is of the essence in a real estate deal. Remember, a good agent will save you time, effort, energy, and money, and will be able to negotiate for you more effectively because they are not emotionally involved.

For investors like Jim, emotion never enters the picture. Every deal has to meet his criteria and his formula: a 70 percent loan-to-value ratio, a 15-year note, and a rental rate that's more than his monthly payment including taxes. His rule of thumb—never buy a home you have to "take a negative on." If the numbers don't work, he walks away—even if he has to make 10 offers before he can close 1 deal.

The only time Jim got into trouble was when he bought an investment with terms, paid too much, and the market shifted. Follow his advice and be sure to make money going in. Meeting your property and financial criteria and starting with positive cash flow are good minimum goals to make a smart investment. Your agent will help you accomplish these with a well-thought-out offer letter.

But to get to that final offer letter to the seller, you and your agent will go through three steps.

1. Write the Offer

2. Bulletproof the Offer

3. Present the Offer

We'll walk you through each in the following few pages.

1. WRITE THE OFFER

Most real estate agents have standardized forms promulgated by the local real estate authority that they can use as the basis for structuring your offer letter. A typical offer letter starts by identifying the basics—buyer, seller, property location, brokers—then it details the purchase price offered, the down payment, the loan amount, and the deposit. It includes time limits for responding to the offer, for obtaining financing, for closing on the home, and for taking possession. In the next few sections, we'll discuss these and other items your offer should include.

When you make your official offer or bid, you need to keep in mind that it could easily become a legally binding contract. Therefore, you need to make sure the offer includes all the contingencies, concessions, and other details you need it to cover in a legally enforceable document. If you're lucky enough to live in a state that has what's called an option period—you get to put the house under contract and only lose a couple hundred dollars if you decide to walk away within a week to ten days—you should get the property under contract quickly.

Otherwise, talk to your agent about including special contingency clauses to protect you. We'll cover these in the next step, "Bulletproof the Offer," in more detail.

The rule of thumb, when it comes to timing is ideally you want to be the first or last to make an offer. Again, the two things you'll want solidified prior to writing your offer are price and terms.

Name Your Price

By the time you make an offer on the property, you should already know what comparable properties are selling for. Your agent should also know what a fair price is for your target property. They will be able to provide you with a comparative market analysis, showing statistics of list prices vs. sales prices for the neighborhood, and compare the prices and quality of other properties with the one that you wish to purchase.

When establishing your offer price, it's very helpful to find out why the house is being sold and whether the seller is under pressure. Austin agent Gene Arant, who has a record of successful transactions representing both buyers and sellers, offers this advice: "First, have your agent run a history report on the property and find out how much the seller paid for it," Gene says. Let's say he bought the property in 1999 for $203,000 and he's asking $300,000. You check the public records, pull the tax report, and see that the seller refinanced the property in 2008, so they now owe $210,000. Knowing that the seller has $90,000 in equity can be used to your advantage.

"Next, have your agent call the seller's agent and try to find out why they're selling. Although the seller's agent cannot disclose information without the client's consent, they may do it to entice an offer. Find out if the seller is facing a job transfer, if they have already purchased a new home, or if they are divorcing. If it's an estate, the heirs may have positive or negative emotional ties to the property. You look at the number of days that it's been on the market. Every month a vacant house remains unsold represents considerable extra expense for the seller. Has the price been reduced? Have they gotten any offers on the property? All of these facts help to create a picture of a seller and give you more bargaining power."

Three Things Every Investor Wants to Know About the Seller

1. Reason: Why are they moving?
2. Time Line: When are they moving?
3. Flexibility: Will they accept terms?

Figure 10-1

As any good real estate agent will tell you, the more you can find out about the seller's needs, the better chance you have to find solutions that appeal to their deepest concerns. The goal is to get the home at the best possible price without insulting the seller. By making an unrealistic offer on a house that is priced correctly and meets your needs, you could end up forfeiting a great opportunity.

After running sales comps in the Springfield neighborhood for both prospects and talking to their agents, you find out that the single-family homeowner is selling due to a job opportunity and has already moved. This means they are probably what we call a motivated seller, and the likelihood of getting the 10 percent discount on your purchase price of $150,000 is good. Comparatively, you find out the duplex is on the market due to a divorce. But since it is still cash flowing—remember, both units are currently occupied—the sellers do not seem as encouraged to sell quickly. On the other hand, the comps do line up with the FMV of $205,000 as opposed to the list price of $210,000.

Since you've gotten some additional insight on both properties, you will want to revisit your terms and discuss matters with your agent prior to making an offer.

Know Your Terms

In real estate, there are two types of buyers—those who have cash and those who don't. Having cash or financing in hand gives you more leverage to negotiate. Cash is king, and there's a premium for having it—sometimes leading to a fairly significant discount on the asking price.

There are many reasonable requests you might make with an offer other than discounting the purchase price. For instance, you may ask the seller to contribute to closing costs, or to provide a home warranty in case something wrong is not detected during escrow or goes wrong in the following year. You could ask for sixty days to secure financing and then set a date for the seller to be out of the property. You may also ask for assistance on the prorating of taxes, club dues, homeowners association fees, and so on.

Even if you don't have cash, you may be able to negotiate terms that will help make the deal more attractive to both you and the seller. We know investors who have structured terms using alternative forms of collateral, such as CDs, stock portfolios, cars, or jewelry. Anything of value that you own free and clear may be an acceptable form of collateral.

You can also arrange terms that will make your offer more attractive to the seller. For instance, if the seller needs to move within a certain period of time, you can offer to close quickly. Or, if the seller is an investor and has capital gains considerations, you can escrow the money and wait to close until it's more convenient for them. The goal is to find out what the seller's hot buttons are and use them to your advantage.

Maybe they have to move within some set period of time because they've bought another house. Maybe they can't afford to meet their payments or make needed repairs. In this case, your first question to the seller should be, "Does it have to be cash or can we have terms?"

"You always have to look at the seller's situation to see what strategy will work for them because not all strategies will work for every situation," Wendy Patton advises. "Once I know that it works for the seller, I have to know if it works for me as an investor. What can I offer to the seller that's going to make the deal good for me and good for them?"

For example, on a past deal, Patton made an offer on a property for $215,000 on a lease option with a monthly payment of $1,200. The owners were retiring and moving to a house they had bought on the other side of Michigan. They had lived in their previous home for thirty-five years—it was the only home they ever owned—and had concerns about the transaction. Patton went to the home, sat down with the couple, and asked them what they were thinking.

When Patton asked what her concerns were, the wife replied, "I just want to be done with this house. I don't want to see it or deal with it ever again." After further probing they revealed that her offer of $1,200 per month was $40 short of the monthly note. The couple told her that if she would make the mortgage payment of $1,240 a month, she could buy the house for what they owed: $181,000. By simply talking to the seller, she was able to find out what their real needs were and saved $34,000!

You may not always be able to do this. In fact, it's not out of the norm for sellers to be slightly close-lipped. But, again, it's worth asking. Figure 10-2 condenses the known information that could be useful in negotiating terms for both Springfield properties.

Useful Information for Terms on Springfield Prospects		
	742 Evergreen Terrace (SFH)	**127 Elm Street (Duplex)**
Why Selling	Career Opportunity	Divorce
When Moving	Already Moved	No Set Time, Currently Occupied
Cash or Terms	Either	Cash

Figure 10-2

Based on the information in figure 10-2, it appears the single-family home might line up with your criteria a bit more closely. But, we'll say it again: It doesn't hurt to try with the duplex as well. The worst that can happen is your offer will be denied, at which point you can reassess and make a second offer or simply walk away.

Regardless of which property you decide to go with, there are a few ways to bulletproof your offer. You should discuss these with your agent before submitting anything to the seller.

2. BULLETPROOF THE OFFER

As an investor, you want to include certain conditions, or contingencies, that will protect you in the event that you need to renegotiate the deal. Contingencies limit the buyer's or seller's responsibility to fulfill the contract in the event that some unforeseen incident occurs.

For example, a buyer might want to make their purchase contingent upon their ability to obtain financing. Another buyer may want to make his offer contingent on the home appraising at (or above) the purchase price. Buyers will often want to make the purchase contingent on whether the property passes various inspections.

Gene Arant, the Austin agent, cautions that you should go slowly before including too many contingencies in your offer—especially if the property is already a good deal. "The cleaner the offer, the better you can do on price," he said. "Sellers don't like a lot of contingencies. And if you're serious about the property, you don't want to give them too many outs. If the price is low enough, you may be willing to take a risk in order to avoid losing an excellent opportunity."

However, there are some reasonable contingencies you may want to include in your offer:

- **Home inspection**: In most states, the seller is obligated under law to disclose all known defects of the property in written form as part of the purchase contract. Since the inspection may take place after the offer is accepted, you need to state in the contract that the entire deal is contingent upon an acceptable inspection report. If an inspection turns up termites, roof problems, or major structural damage, make sure there is a clear contingency in the purchase contract that states any defects in the home must be either repaired or monetarily compensated for. If you are not satisfied, you have the option to cancel the contract.

  In addition to the home inspection, you may also want to check to see what sorts of permits have been issued for the property. Permits can tell a lot about any work that has been done to the home in the past. Don't wait until you have placed an offer on a house before you begin the search for a home inspector. There will be a time limit in the contract designating when the inspection must be completed—typically from three to fourteen days, depending on the house and the market area.

- **Financing contingencies**: You may want to include a contingency for obtaining specific financing from a lending institution. If the loan can't be found, you won't be bound by the contract.

- **Items included in the purchase**: This can include major appliances, lighting fixtures, shrubbery, and anything else that the seller might take with them. Basically, if it's not nailed down and you want it included in the purchase, list it.

- **Title contingencies**: Your attorney or title company will do a title search to make sure the property does not have any legal claims against it and that the seller holds a clear title to it. Your offer may want to include a contingency based on this, stating that if the title is found to be "cloudy," you are free to walk away.

- **Time line**: A deadline for responding so you know when to consider the offer rejected is also a good idea. When writing an offer, one should allow three days for the seller to respond.

3. PRESENT THE OFFER

Reviewing and presenting an offer is one of the most critical steps in purchasing an investment property. But, before you do sit down with your agent for one final review, make sure you haven't missed any details or opportunities as there is a lot at stake.

In the end, you'll want to have your agent present on your behalf and see if the seller counteroffers. We look at offers like a tennis match—negotiations may, and oftentimes do, take place here for the first time. We always want the ball to end up on the seller's side of the net.

The word "negotiation" may conjure images of hostage standoffs and high-stakes business deals. In reality, it is a conversation between two or more points of view that seeks to move the parties away from opposite positions and into a place of mutual interest.

Negotiations will typically take place after you present your initial offer, but it is important to be aware of when, where, and how they might occur on both sides. Usually, the buyer will make an initial offer, at which point the seller will accept, decline, or counter. This is where the dance begins. If the seller counters your offer, you and your agent will review their proposal and volley back with an acceptance, denial, or counter. This usually only goes back and forth once, but it can reemerge again during inspections, etc. Either way, it's important to be aware of what you're negotiating.

Some people will ask for everything in a negotiation, but at a certain point you can personally insult and alienate the seller. As a buyer, you need to be able to strike a balance between what you want and what the seller wants. For the seller, it's almost always, "When am I going to close and how much am I going to net?" For the buyer, it's, "How much money will I have to bring to the table, and how much will the property cash flow?" You don't want to be out-negotiated and buy a property that isn't a good HOLD investment because of the price or terms. On the other hand, you don't want to nitpick the sellers to the point that they walk away from the table and you have to search for another six months to find a suitable property, where with a few minor concessions on your part, you could have closed the deal.

Linda McKissack refers to such shortsighted thinking as stepping over dollars to get dimes. A better way to negotiate is to find out what the motivations of the other person are and try to meet them without losing sight of your own goals. This way, you can achieve a win-win outcome.

After you are prepared for possible negotiations, there are a few more final considerations:

- Use a standard offer letter to outline the terms of the deal.

- Include a negotiated option period during which the contract must be executed. This gives you time to inspect the property and make sure it is what it was presented to be. If you terminate at any time during the option period, your earnest money will be refunded. If you go to closing, that money will apply to the closing costs.

- If you're buying a property that's already rented, the contract should stipulate that the rents are prorated to the close of escrow and the deposit monies are turned over to the buyer.

- Reserve the right to inspect and bring contractors in to get bids during the escrow period to see if there's any work to be done.

As you can see, though time is of the essence in a real estate deal, it's important to cross your t's and dot your i's. This is a legally binding contract and you definitely do not want to end up belly-up.

For instance, you've closely examined both Springfield properties at this point and come up with an offer for each. The single-family on Evergreen Terrace accepted your offer of $135,000, whereas the duplex on Elm denied your offer of $184,500. Rather than continuing the negotiation tennis match that could have ensued with the duplex, you decided to walk away and move forward with the single-family.

Congratulations! You're buying a HOLD investment! Now it's time to seal the deal and close on the property.

POINTS TO REMEMBER

- Every real estate transaction has two areas of negotiation: price and terms. If you give up something on price, you should always seek to make it back on the terms.

- When making your official offer, always keep in mind that it could easily become a legally binding contract. Therefore, you need to include all of the contingencies, concessions, and other details that will protect you in a legally enforceable document.

- When establishing your offer price, you should first consider the comps and then the seller's motivation. A motivated seller may be willing to discount the price or agree to more advantageous terms.

- There is no "one size fits all" strategy of negotiating a real estate contract. Meet the seller face-to-face, be pleasant, and listen. The goal is to structure a deal that's in both parties' best interests.

CHAPTER 11: CLOSE THE PURCHASE

> ✓ **1. FIND**
> The right property for the right terms and the right price

Outcome: a list of qualified investment properties from which to choose
↓

> ✓ **2. ANALYZE**
> A property to make sure the numbers and the terms make sense

Outcome: a prospect that meets your financial criteria
↓

> **3. BUY**
> An investment property where you make money going in
> ☑ **Chapter 9**: Arrange Financing
> ☑ **Chapter 10**: Write and Present the Offer
> ☐ **Chapter 11**: Close the Purchase

↓
Outcome: a profitable property to add to your HOLD investment portfolio

---

After reading this chapter, you will know how to:

☐ Prepare yourself in advance for a successful closing.

☐ Use the inspection process to gain knowledge of your investment.

☐ Avoid potential pitfalls and close without delay.

Closing is a term used for the point in time at which the title to the property is transferred to the buyer who places a mortgage (or "deed of trust") with the lender. The process begins from the minute the seller accepts your offer and continues until the documentation is signed and recorded.

Timing is critical to make sure all the elements for a successful closing are in place. A closing agent—which may be a title company, escrow company, or attorney, depending on your place of residence—will handle the closing and the legal transfer of title and ownership. Since the seller typically pays for the title policy, they usually name the closing agent, but this is always open for negotiation. Do your best.

You may want to follow Jim's example and use the same agent for all your closings. His title company is an important part of his HOLD investment team. The company maintains all his documents and understands how he wants the deal to be structured. They do lien searches on prospective properties and check back taxes. More than just closing the deal, his title company is a trusted partner, simplifying and smoothing the process and giving him peace of mind.

Once your closing agent is selected, he or she will handle the closing process from that point on. The sections below go over the various preclosing and closing activities and what to expect at each stage.

PREPARE TO CLOSE

Before a transaction can be cleared for closing, there are many steps that take place to solidify the deal. This is when you will get all of your questions answered and ducks in a row prior to signing. There are several processes to help you check off on your purchase decision, such as inspection, title search, insurance quotes, and more.

Get a Home Inspection

The purchase agreement usually calls for a home inspection to evaluate the physical condition, structure, and mechanical systems of the house. A licensed inspector will conduct a detailed analysis and prepare a report detailing their findings. In fact, according to the American Society of Home Inspectors (ASHI), there are ten areas the inspection will focus on, as shown in figure 11-1.

Ten Focal Points of a Home Inspection

1. Structural, both foundation and framing

2. Exterior, including wall coverings, flashings, trim, grading, decks, patios, and balconies

3. Roofing, including flashings, skylights, chimneys, and roof penetration

4. Plumbing, including water supply, drainage, and water-heating system

5. Electrical, including conductors, cables, lighting fixtures/switches, and ground fault circuit interrupters

6. Heating

7. Air-conditioning

8. Interior walls, ceilings, floors, stairways, railings, doors, windows, etc.

9. Insulation and ventilation, including unfinished spaces and attics

10. Fireplace and solid fuel-burning appliances

Figure 11-1

Although you are not required to be present at the home inspection, it is a good idea for you to be there. This is your opportunity to learn about the structure of the house, its systems, what to look out for to prevent costly repairs or replacements, and what to do in an emergency.

The inspection is a great opportunity to renegotiate. The biggest things to look for in a home inspection are problems with the roof, foundation, and air-conditioning. If issues are found, share the report with the seller and ask them to either make the repairs, pay equivalent closing costs, or make other concessions. Some big repairs—such as faulty foundation—will be required by the lender. The rest are a matter of negotiation. A good rule of thumb here is to ask the seller to handle serious repairs like plumbing, foundation, or electrical work. Anytime you peel back the drywall, you risk uncovering other problems. You want those new issues—think mold, hidden cracked pipes, or termites—to be their problem. For cosmetic work, fixtures, and other issues that hold less risk, we suggest gathering estimates on larger fixes and asking for the cash amount off of the purchase price, so that you can use your own team of professionals for the repairs.

Appraise the Property

An appraisal is different from a home inspection. An appraiser will inspect the property, verifying that it is worth as much or more than the purchase price. The property will be compared to others in the area with similar size, style, and features. Lenders have approved appraisers that they like to use. If there is a disagreement on the appraised value of the property, you can order an independent appraisal. Of course, there is only a red flag if the appraisal turns up lower than the originally agreed-upon purchase price. In this case, the bank will not lend you the higher amount and you'll want to renegotiate.

Order a Title Search

The title company will search legal records to establish whether the seller is the true owner of the property under contract and determine if there are any legal or financial issues that may affect your ownership of the property. Such issues can be things like pending litigation, back taxes, first and second mortgages, debt, and mechanical liens. Any problems with the title need to be addressed before closing. This becomes even more critical when you're buying a foreclosure. Foreclosures are more likely than most properties to have liens or judgments against them, and you only have a limited period of time to do a search. Therefore, it's a good idea to have a relationship with a title company you can trust to do the search quickly and accurately.

Your lender will also require you to buy title insurance on the property at this time. This will protect you and the lender from ownership claims that may arise later. A lot of titles are "cloudy," especially in markets where there are a large number of foreclosures. Title insurance will protect you against this.

Get the Survey

The lender will ask for a survey of the property to verify its boundaries. A professional survey will help you understand your legal rights to the property and what comes with it, such as a driveway, yard, or fence. Oftentimes, this is something buyers will ask the seller to pay for in the closing terms. One of the main issues to look for on the survey would be anomalies like a fence or structure that extends beyond the property lines, or a utility or other easement that would prevent you from building structures or additions to a property.

Nail Down Insurance

We briefly discussed homeowners insurance in the Analyze section. This is the time you'll want to make sure you've received several quotes and picked an insurance carrier. Again, using the same provider for your home and car insurance will likely get you a discounted rate. Similarly, your driving record, level of education, and length of time with the company can do the same.

A few tips in deciding on a carrier are to make sure the company has a local branch, to introduce yourself to a branch representative and decide if you want to do business together. Discuss your coverage at length and make sure you understand all of your options. Depending on your other assets, you may want to look into an umbrella policy as an extra layer of protection.

Schedule a Final Walk-Through

Many buyers will schedule a final walk-through within twenty-four hours of closing, assuming this option is specified in the purchase contract. This is your opportunity to check out the house to make sure it is in the condition you and the seller agreed upon in the contract. Any problems discovered previously that the seller agreed to fix should already be corrected. If any major problems are found during the final walk-through, you can ask to delay the closing or request that the seller deposit money into an escrow account to cover the necessary repairs. Sometimes the seller may offer to reduce the purchase price of the property instead of delaying closing. If this happens, your lender will need to get involved in case this impacts the appraised value of the property.

FINALIZE THE TRANSACTION

After you've lined everything up—inspection, final negotiations, title, survey, and insurance—it's time to close! Yes, get excited! You're in the final phase to buying your HOLD investment property. Again, congrats!

Closings usually take place at the office of either the title company or the attorney handling the transaction. At this time the buyer and seller will sign the legal documents that officially transfer title. During the meeting, the closing agent will verify that all documents are properly signed and collect all necessary payments. The agent will be responsible for recording the legal documents and making sure that escrow payments are distributed properly.

Along with escrow payments, there will be some other costs associated with closing. Some information about these costs should be provided to you before you put a contract on a house. If you are obtaining a loan to purchase the property, your lender has three days from the time of the loan application to provide you with a good faith estimate of your loan costs so there are no surprises.

The amount of closing costs varies but may include points, a loan origination fee, an appraisal fee, the cost of a credit report, a lender's inspection fee, the cost of title insurance, a mortgage broker fee, taxes, and a fee for document preparation.

At the closing, you will receive the following documentation to sign and verify your final transactions—financial or otherwise:

- **Truth in Lending Act (TILA) Disclosure Statement**, revealing all costs of financing the home, detailing interest expense, and discount points.

- **HUD Settlement Statement**, a precise disclosure of the final closing costs and financial details of the transaction, including real estate commissions and initial escrow amounts.

- **Mortgage Note**, outlining the terms and conditions of the buyer's promise to repay the loan.

- **Deed of Trust**, securing the mortgage note and giving the lender legal claim to foreclose on the property should the buyer neglect to honor the terms of the mortgage agreement.

Once all papers are signed at the closing table, the lender funds the closing and the title is officially transferred from the seller to the buyer. You will be given keys and will officially own your HOLD investment property. Now the fun really begins. In the next segment, "Manage," we'll walk you through finding good tenants for the single-family on 742 Evergreen Terrace, increasing your property value, and maintaining good records in preparation to expand your HOLD investments in the future.

For now, cheers! Take a minute to celebrate and pat yourself on the back for all of your hard work up to this point. You've put in the time, effort, and energy, and you've made a great HOLD investment. You're officially on the path to a better financial future, and you should be proud.

POINTS TO REMEMBER

- The closing process begins from the minute the seller accepts your offer and continues until the documentation is signed and recorded.

- Timing is critical to make sure all elements for a successful closing are in place. Work with an experienced closing agent with a solid reputation. A good agent can be an investor's trusted partner, simplifying and smoothing the process and providing peace of mind.

- Schedule your housing inspection in advance. When you're trying to close a deal in a competitive situation, it's no time to start looking for a reputable housing inspector.

- Check the house within twenty-four hours of closing. If you find a problem, don't hesitate to bring it up before closing.

- Prior to closing, make sure the closing agent has everything he or she needs. Don't run the risk of delays because the agent is missing some critical piece of documentation.

STAGE 4: MANAGE

✓ ## 1. FIND
The right property for the right terms and the right price

Outcome: a list of qualified investment properties from which to choose

↓

✓ ## 2. ANALYZE
A property to make sure the numbers and the terms make sense

Outcome: a prospect that meets your financial criteria

↓

✓ ## 3. BUY
An investment property where you make money going in

Outcome: a profitable property to add to your HOLD investment portfolio

↓

4. MANAGE
Your tenants and properties like a pro

☐ **Chapter 12**: Find Good Tenants

☐ **Chapter 13**: Increase Value

☐ **Chapter 14**: Run It Like a Business

↓

Outcome: a sustainable investment property for your HOLD portfolio

The best education in operations, particularly in the early stages of ownership, is actually managing an apartment house.

WILLIAM NICKERSON

Now that you have purchased your first investment property, you are entering a new phase of your HOLD journey: that of investment property owner. But owning a property and managing it isn't the same thing. Some investors steer clear of property management and focus all their efforts on generating leads and acquiring properties. That's fine. If your cash flow allows for a professional property manager, this can be a great choice. Still, wherever your wealth is, you should be there too. You'll still need to understand the process at a working level so you can hold your property manager accountable to keeping your property rented and well maintained. Many investors actively engage in managing their properties, especially in the beginning of their investment career, either to save money or gain valuable experience. This is a great choice too. Nothing replaces on-the-job learning and you can always engage a professional property manager at a later date.

Either way, you need to think of this as a small business, and just like any small business owner, you must be organized, professional, detail oriented, financially astute, and fiscally prudent. In short, all the skills that have brought you this far should serve you well as a landlord and property manager.

For our purposes, we'll write from the perspective that you've chosen to dive in head first and actively manage 742 Evergreen Terrace. We'll cover prepping the property for lease and then finding a great tenant. We'll explore different ways to add value to your investment and finish with a quick overview of how-tos—records, bookkeeping, etc.—of running it like a business. There is a lot of ground to cover.

Your duties will run the gamut from advertising your property to finding tenants, establishing rental rates and lease agreements, complying with local housing laws, dealing with rental collections—and possibly evictions—and handling major repairs and upgrades. Not to mention all the minor mishaps such as clogged drains, leaky faucets, and broken fixtures.

Being a landlord will require you to wear many hats: marketer, manager, accountant, handyman, and, most important, customer service professional. Although you may not think of it this way, your property is your product and your tenants are your customers. By establishing and maintaining excellent customer relationships, you will ensure quality tenants who take care of your property, pay the rent on time, and, when it's time for them to move, recommend you to friends looking for a place to live.

Although it will take some added time and effort, it's important to remember not to let it take over your life. If you're like most HOLD investors, you're likely to have a full-time "day job" outside of your real estate investing activities. So it's important to strike a balance. Investment property management tends to come in bursts. There is a lot to do in the beginning, when new tenants are needed and obviously when repairs are too. Depending on the demands of your primary job, managing a property or two should not be an issue. Still, we've known investors who've unnecessarily let their investments run their lives. Don't join that club. Periodically, assess the time you are willing and able to give and make a conscious decision about whether hiring a property manager is right for you. This is one of the reasons we advocated finding properties that cash flowed enough to include a property manager. Life happens. You might get a promotion or have a major change in your homelife (say, having a child) and want to hand over the reins for altogether positive reasons. Because you acquired your property with sound HOLD criteria, this will always be your option.

Most of all, remember that being a landlord can be very rewarding! Yes, it can be challenging at times, but as a landlord you play an important role that goes beyond your personal investment goals. You not only support the welfare of your tenants, but also your community by increasing property values and improving the quality of life. By committing to managing your property as a business with professionalism and pride, you can build a solid, sustainable, and successful investment portfolio.

In this section, we'll provide you with tools, systems, and processes to help you get off to a great start and increase your chances of finding the right tenant, handling day-to-day maintenance, and keeping your new business running smoothly and profitably.

CHAPTER 12: FIND GOOD TENANTS

√ **3. BUY**
An investment property where you make money going in

Outcome: a profitable property to add to your HOLD investment portfolio

↓

4. MANAGE
Your tenants and properties like a pro

☐ **Chapter 12**: Find Good Tenants

☐ **Chapter 13**: Increase Value

☐ **Chapter 14**: Run It Like a Business

↓

Outcome: a sustainable investment property for your HOLD portfolio

After reading this chapter, you will know how to:

☐ Set the rent.

☐ Promote your property.

☐ Show and lease the property.

☐ Manage a flawless move-in.

You found the location, analyzed the property, made your offer, and bought the single-family home on 742 Evergreen Terrace. Now the fun really begins. Welcome to the wonderful and wacky world of property management!

Steve Chader and Jennice Doty are partners in a property management firm that oversees more than 1,000 residential properties throughout Arizona. With thirty years' experience in this arena, Jennice has seen and heard it all, but every now and then she is still surprised.

There was the family that apparently loved all things fried. When they moved out, the grease in the kitchen was half an inch thick. Then there was the "Scorpion Queen" who kept finding scorpions no matter how often the exterminator came. After moving out, she mailed in an envelope of 16 scorpion carcasses. There were even reports of a haunted property that culminated in a request for an exorcism.

The good news is 99 percent of tenants are perfectly pleasant and easy to deal with. In fact, throughout the years, we have converted a number of former renters to owners of one of our properties and have been quite pleased with the outcome. However, there will be a few exceptions, and those can cost you endless amounts of time, energy, and money. So, as with every step of your HOLD journey thus far, put forth extra effort on the front end to avoid anxiety on the tail end.

To help you do just that, we're going to walk through how to set your rent, market your property to attract the largest pool of qualified tenants, screen tenants, and execute a lease that protects your interests. We'll also touch on how to navigate the day-to-day challenges and rewards that come with owning and managing any rental property.

SET THE RENT

During the Analyze phase, you pulled rental comps to project the rent for 742 Evergreen Terrace. That figure ended up being $1,390, which you used in your HOLD Property Analysis Worksheet. Considering it has likely been a month or longer since you did your analysis, ask your real estate agent or property manager to pull any recent comps that might impact your rental rate. This may seem like overkill, but it's good business. Real estate markets can shift suddenly. One month, there are relatively few properties in your area available for rent and landlords can pick and choose from a large pool of renters. From the time you make your offer to the time you close, that scenario can flip all the way to the renters' market. A local apartment building could unexpectedly advertise that it has 100 renovated units ready to rent with a hefty move-in incentive ... suddenly, you have a lot of competition for renters.

Our point? Never assume the market is static. Pull the comps, drive the comps, and make sure your projected rent is competitive.

Even when you do the hard work of surveying the competitive landscape, you may still miss the mark. Don't fret. Listen to what the market is telling you. When renters call about your property, see it, but rent elsewhere, your rent is likely on target but the condition of your property isn't. Spruce it up or lower the rent. If no one is calling at all, you've probably priced it above the market. Start ratcheting down the rent until you find the sweet spot. Even $50 less a month can make a big difference to prospective tenants and get the ball rolling. You want to get the most for your property, but not if that means it stays vacant for several months. Every day it sits vacant, it costs you money. We know from firsthand experience that it's best to price it right with a goal of getting multiple people interested so you can choose the best applicant and rent it quickly.

The rental market is just like the sales market, or any market for that matter, it follows the basic laws of supply and demand. If you pay attention and rely on the help of experienced professionals, most investors find they can do a good job of estimating fair market rents and maximizing the value of their investment. You will too. With that in mind, let's look at the best ways to promote your rental property to attract the largest possible pool of quality renters.

PROMOTE THE PROPERTY

You won't get a tenant if no one knows your property is for rent. Effective targeted marketing along with competitive pricing will drive interest in your property and provide a larger pool of prospective tenants from which to choose. It's a good idea to investigate your target market and advertise in media related to that market. For example, if you have a property that is close to a college, try advertising in the campus paper or posting signs on the community boards. Advertising doesn't need to be complicated or expensive. In fact, some of the best advertising is usually the simplest. Here are some of the methods we've found that seem to work best.

1. Yard Signs

One of the most cost-effective forms of advertising for your rental property is yard signs. In our own surveys of how tenants find rental opportunities, roughly half of them said they saw the sign in the front yard. You can pick up a preprinted "For Rent" sign at your local hardware or stationery story or at online retailers like Amazon.com. If you list the property for rent with a real estate agent or property manager, they will provide their own signs.

For your own signage, just remember to keep the message simple. Include your telephone number and, if you've listed it on an online rentals site, the web address of your listing. And be careful about the sign placement. Don't just stick it in the front yard and forget about it. If a car parks in front of the property and blocks the sign's view from the street, you could lose out on valuable marketing opportunities. Maximize your exposure by adding another sign on the porch or in a front window.

Figure 12-1

You can also take a page from your real estate agent and post directional signs on nearby streets that have good traffic. You've probably seen them for open houses in your own neighborhood. And there is a reason—they work. Just be a good neighbor and always ask the owner for permission to place your sign in their yard. Otherwise, you may find your directional signs in the trash.

Some investors post bandit signs, or simple hand-printed fliers, on telephone poles at intersections. This can also be effective, but check your local ordinances. There is a reason they are called "bandit signs"—they are often illegal. While no one is likely to get ticketed for posting a sign about a garage sale or a lost pet, "For Rent" signs are decidedly commercial in nature and are not likely to be looked upon as kindly.

2. Internet and Social Media

If you don't want to incur costs, the Internet is a very easy DIY listing service and should be at the top of your marketing strategy. In the past, most renters depended on newspaper ads and drive-by signs to find rental property. Today, the majority of renters are going online to sites like Craigslist.org, Rentals.com, or SpeedyTenants.com to find apartments even before they move to a city. Many of the better sites offer multiple photos, virtual tours, maps, and brochure printing. Some investors will also post a listing on their Facebook page or other social media marketing sites. This is not only to catch potential tenants' eyes, but also to alert their network of friends, family, and colleagues to their vacancy.

3. Local and Community Newspaper Ads

Advertise in your local Sunday paper when people have more time to read the ads. And don't forget your neighborhood's weekly. Your prospective tenants may already be renting in the area and looking to upgrade. Prime times to advertise are the first and last weekends of each month when tenants usually give their notice.

With this form of marketing, it's important to stand out. Be creative and have fun with your print ad. Think about who you are trying to reach, and then fashion a headline that will attract that eye.

Take 742 Evergreen Terrace, for example. If it's a younger couple you're looking to rent to, you might want to appeal to their sense of romance.

```
                    Enchanted Cottage

Adorable 3-br., 2-bath bungalow on a tree-lined street.
W/D/Central AC. Close to shopping and entertainment.
$1,390 per mo. plus utilities.
Call for an appointment: 555-4444.
```

Figure 12-2

Whereas a family might respond more to something that addresses their immediate concerns.

```
           2 Blocks from John Adams Elementary!

Spacious, spotless 3-br., 2-bath with fenced yard.
Park, playground nearby. W/D/ Central AC.
$1,390 per mo. plus utilities.
Call for an appointment: 555-4444.
```

Figure 12-3

And, finally, a college student has very different priorities.

```
              Roommate Heaven

2-br., 2-bath with study on the Red Line,
five minutes from campus.
Clean, quiet, secure, all appliances included.
$1,390 per mo. plus utilities.
Call for an appointment: 555-4444.
```

Figure 12-4

Think about your target audience, what they're looking for, and how your property will meet their needs. Then fashion an ad that quickly and effectively communicates this.

4. List with an Agent

As discussed previously, another option is to list your property with a rental agent who will place your home on the MLS. This method may cost a little more in real estate agent fees, but it will give you more prospects to choose from, improving your chances of finding a great tenant and the highest rent. Another bonus is that sometimes the listing agent will include showing the property as part of his fee. This takes the time commitment off of your shoulders until it has been narrowed to a few great prospects. The other obvious advantage is when you put it on the MLS you expose it to every agent in the area with a potential tenant. It may seem worth it to try and save money by not using an agent, but if your property is vacant for even a few weeks, any savings is lost.

5. Fliers and Brochures

Fliers and brochures are another great way to find prospective tenants. If you're handy with a computer or have access to a print or office supply shop, one of these can be an effective and surprisingly affordable marketing tool for properties—especially high-end homes, where you want to feature the landscape, locale, or craftsmanship. Be sure to include the property's features, amenities, and your contact information. The more professional looking the flier or brochure, the better. A professional appearance attracts good tenants and discourages bad ones. Get at least 100 copies made and deliver them door-to-door in the neighborhood. If there's an apartment complex close by, definitely make those rounds, as well as post on local merchants' and businesses' bulletin boards. Sending these in-hand marketing tools to your investor network mailing list is another great option. You can also keep an electronic file of the brochure to email prospective renters.

6. Direct Mail

Develop a mailing list of real estate agents, property managers, friends, family, and other contacts that are part of your investor network. Whenever a property becomes available for rent, you can conduct a coordinated mail campaign of emails, letters, postcards, and even brochures if you have more than one property or a property that may be slower to lease because of price, location, or other factors. You can offer a referral fee if you want to encourage your network to continue sending good tenants your way. Of course, you'll want to do the same when you're asked for prospects on other properties.

You can also purchase targeted demographic or geographic lists to mail to. Just remember to make your campaign stand out if you are going to consider this approach.

7. Open House

If the property is vacant, you may want to hold an open house and make it accessible to the greatest number of prospective tenants. The best time for an open house is Sunday afternoon when people typically drive around looking for properties. Place your ad in the paper that morning so that prospects can see the property the same day. Remember to list all pertinent open house information in your ad and on your voice mail— property specs, address, open house times, price, and all nearby amenities. You'll also want to put up "Open House" signs at nearby intersections and thoroughfares to direct prospects to your property.

Before you schedule your open house, envision how the property will look to fresh eyes. Are the carpets clean? Walls freshly painted? Are the kitchen appliances shiny? When you're showing residential property, it's the seemingly small details that make the difference.

Compare Strategies and Start Promoting

With so many options to choose from, it may seem difficult to narrow down your ad strategy. In all honesty, you'll probably want to use more than one of these techniques to rent your property. Oftentimes, a mixed-media plan is more effective than one-offs. The following Marketing Plan Worksheet in figure 12-5 outlines some of the differences in tools we have found most effective.

For some properties, a yard sign and a Craigslist ad may be all you need to generate a lot of rental applications. For others, you'll need to invest in advertising, the help of a real estate agent, or other methods. Solutions like mailing lists and direct mail are more generally used by investors with more than one property to lease each year. They don't have to weigh the cost of a single campaign against a single stream of income. Finally, ask your HOLD team what they've found to be the most cost-effective ways to generate potential renters in your area. Their local expertise will be invaluable and could save you lots of time, money, and effort.

Marketing Plan Worksheet			
Marketing Tool	**Use**	**Cost**	**Distribution**
1. **Yard Signs**	Capture area residents and drive-bys	$3.00–$50.00	Front yard, windows, directional signs
2. **Internet and Social Media**	Ads on rental and social media sites	Free	Continual runs on various sites
3. **Local and Community Newspaper Ads**	Week/Weekend editions	Call for rates	First and last weekends of the month
4. **List with an Agent**	Post to MLS	Percentage of one month's rent	Leverages established real estate system
5. **Fliers and Brochures**	Detailed information and referral fees	$0.10–$1.50 plus design cost	Fax, email, bulletin boards, mailing lists, open house
6. **Direct Mail**	Used as piece in mail campaign	$0.40–$0.60 including postage	Mailing list
7. **Open House**	High-end or hard-to-rent properties	Varies	Sunday afternoon between 1:00 and 4:00 p.m.

Figure 12-5

SHOW AND LEASE THE PROPERTY

Now that you have a marketing plan in place, it's time to learn the ins and outs of spotting and signing great tenants. There are basically six major steps to leasing and moving in new renters:

1. Show the Property
2. Process the Application
3. Screen the Tenant
4. Review the Lease
5. Sign the Lease and Collect Deposits
6. Move In

Of course there are a myriad of smaller steps that will ensure a smooth leasing transaction, but we will discuss those within each category. You can also use figure 12-6 as a quick go-to reminder guide on all of the steps from leasing to landlord.

1. Show the Property

Most of the time, prospective tenants will want to see the property before they rent it. As we discussed in "Promote the Property," this duty is sometimes built in to your marketing plan—working with an agent and having an open house, for example. However, even if it's not part of the initial strategy, it's important to have the property available for showings. Remember to keep it clean and visible at all times while vacant, and help prospects envision what the remodeled countertops and flooring will look like when complete. When the house is vacant, it's actually easier to show, as you're only dealing with one person's schedule: the interested party. Also, a good

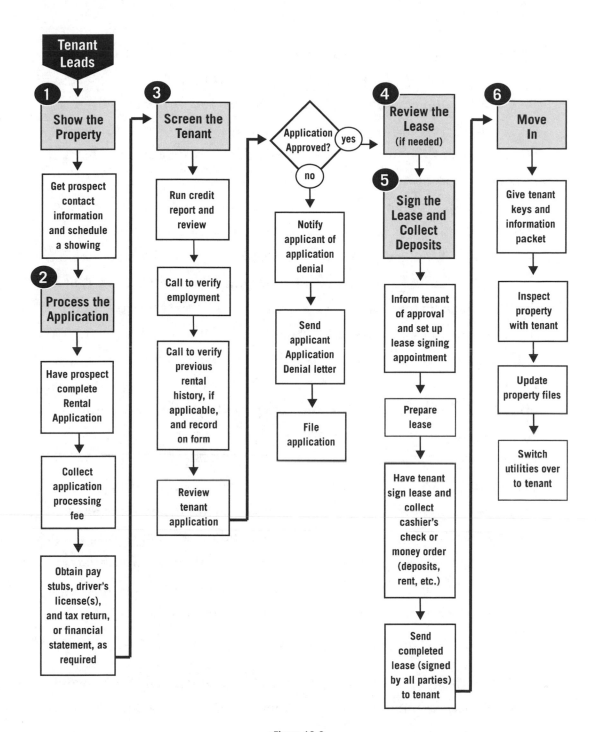

Figure 12-6

way to allow other agents to show the property when vacant is to put a lockbox (available at your local home improvement store and online) on it.

On the flip side of that coin, sometimes the property will not be vacant until a few months after you buy it. If this is the case, you'll need to be courteous of your current tenants and call to schedule an appointment to show the property.

If you are doing extensive repairs or improvements to the property, you'll want to weigh the pros and cons of showing it while the work is being done. Since you now own the property, you'll likely be feeling the pressure of the upcoming mortgage payment and want to rent it quickly. Vacancy has a real cost and you're right to want to minimize it. However, most tenants are renting because they don't want to deal with maintenance and few will be able to envision the property in its finished state when it's still a work zone. If the work is minor—touching up paint or replacing a few fixtures—it's probably okay to move forward with showing the property to interested prospects, especially in a tight market where renters are competing for available vacancies. On the other hand, if you are installing flooring or demoing walls, it's probably best to wait. Renters often see multiple properties in the same day and may opt for a lesser property that's cleaner and neater than yours. Think about it and do your best to see the property through your potential tenant's eyes. In any case, there are a couple of questions you always want to ask interested parties when scheduling an appointment:

- What their name and phone number is.

- When they need to move in—an exact date, if possible. Some people don't need a home for a month or more and you should not hold the property for them.

Always remember safety first. This is not to scare you, but more valuable common sense. You should let someone know that you are going to show a property and an approximate time you will return. If you ever feel uncomfortable about a showing for any reason, ask someone to go with you. It's always better to err on the side of caution.

Aside from this, remember to have fun with your new property. If you love it and it shows, your prospective tenants will too! We've given you some other tips in figure 12-7 to help screen prospects and move on to the processing phase.

Tips to Maximize Leasing Success

1. Schedule two or more prospective tenants to view the property at the same time to optimize your time and avoid no-shows. The prime time to schedule appointments is Monday through Thursday from 5:30 to 6:00 p.m., when prospects are leaving work.

2. Be prepared to answer questions about the property—including utility costs—and have rental applications with you for prospective tenants to fill out.

3. Sell yourself. Even if prospective tenants love a property, they may still walk away from the deal if they have doubts about the landlord. When you're renting a property, unlike selling a home, you're starting a long-term relationship.

4. Meet prospective tenants personally even if you are using a real estate agent. While they are assessing you, you should be assessing them. Listen to your instincts. If they are sounding an alarm, pay attention. Renting to the wrong person is an expensive mistake to make.

5. If you're using a property management firm, you should rely on their expertise to find and negotiate with prospective tenants. You are paying the property manager to serve as the buffer between you and the tenant—if the tenant knows who the owner is, it can make negotiations far more difficult and create more complications when conflicts or requests for rent abatement arise.

Figure 12-7

Once you start to show the property, it should only be a matter of time before you receive some interest. This is why you should always have an application on hand. Think of it as fishing: 742 Evergreen Terrace is the bait, and the application is that initial pull to set the hook. Now you just reel them in to decide if they're a keeper or not.

2. Process the Application

If the prospective tenant indicates that he or she is interested in renting the property, have them complete a rental application and sign it. This document is available online, or you can always ask your agent or other local property managers to share their version with you. The main things to include on the application are prior rental history and agreement for a credit check. Other information you may ask for is work history, vehicle information, or references.

There are online tenant screening agencies that can provide you with a credit report for a reasonable cost. There is of course a fee associated with running a credit check. To cover that cost, we charge an application processing fee of $25. This fee works twofold: 1. It obviously covers the cost of the credit check, and 2. It show genuine interest in the property. If a prospective tenant is not willing to pay the application fee, chances are they're not that interested or you may have trouble collecting other payments from them in the future.

Make sure to collect the application fee in the form of cash, cashier's check, or money order. Checks bounce. You should also obtain copies of pay stubs and driver's licenses for each person on their application. If the applicant is self-employed, you may need to obtain a copy of his/her tax return or financial statement (both if available). This information is very important to both run the credit report as well as to calculate the rent-to-income ratio during application processing.

If there will be two or more people living on the property, you'll need to collect an application from each one. For instance, let's say 742 Evergreen Terrace ended up skewing toward that bungalow for young couples discussed earlier in the chapter. You'd need to collect filled-out applications from both individuals to continue in the processing phase.

3. Screen the Tenant

As we've discussed, choosing your tenants wisely is one of the most critical elements to managing a property. That's why we recommend that you screen all potential tenants thoroughly. Take the time to meet possible renters in person, or have a trusted property manager work as your screening board. And don't let emotions get in the way. Be sure to run a credit, employment, and rental history check before agreeing to rent to someone.

Run a credit report on each of the listed applicants. While you are waiting to receive information, you should call to verify employment, references, and rental history. To verify employment information, make sure to write down the name of the employee who you spoke with and their title, dates of employment, and verified income (if necessary). For rental history, contact any prior landlords or places of residence listed on the application to find out dates rented, rental amounts, and whether the landlords would rent to the person again.

Once the credit report has been received, review it to ensure that the information listed on the application matches that on the credit report. If the information on the credit report and employer verifications do not match, you should be very cautious about approving the application without further investigation. Judgments, bankruptcies, and criminal reports are indicated on the credit report and should also be warning flags regarding the creditworthiness of an applicant.

When renting a lower-end property, you'll find a credit check to be less useful. Many if not most candidates applying for this tier of housing will have poor to no credit. In these cases, you'll want to rely more on alternate screening methods—references from previous landlords and employers, for example.

In areas where there has been a real estate recession, bear in mind that many otherwise solid applicants may have poor credit because of a short sale (where they had to sell the home for less than they owed) or a foreclosure (where they defaulted on a mortgage they could no longer afford). Good people do become victims to bad markets, poor financial choices in their youth, or other financial hardships, the most common of which is a personal bankruptcy resulting from medical expenses or a prolonged period of unemployment. These prospects can sometimes be on a mission to reform their finances and the last thing they would do is miss a rent payment.

In these cases, it's also helpful to calculate the rent-to-income ratio. The rule of thumb here is that the tenant's rent should be no more than 33 percent of their annual income. To find this number, you simply divide the monthly rent by the prospect's monthly income. If there are two incomes, simply add them together first and then divide.

Following our earlier "couple's bungalow" hypothetical, let's say you are screening John and Alida, a young couple just moving to Springfield to start their careers. John works in the HR department of a corporate office and Alida works at the local library. John's annual salary is $41,500 and Alida's is $30,000, so together they make about $5,958 per month. Of course this is before taxes, so the rent expense should be far lower than the 33 percent mark.

742 Evergreen Terrace Example

Couple's Income: $3,458 + $2,500 = $5,958

Rent-to-Income Ratio: $1,390/$5,958 = 23.33 percent

The moral is that when it comes to dealing with people, anything can happen—in spite of your best precautions. But it's important to take extra time during the screening process to try and get a sense of who your possible tenants are before approving the application.

Though John and Alida can afford the Springfield property, they are young and haven't built much credit yet. Therefore, it's important to call their previous landlords and references to make sure they are in fact reliable renters. It is also possible to charge a higher security deposit to offset the risk of a tenant that has no credit or even some "dings" on their credit report.

4. Review the Lease

Of course, during the application process, you'll also need to make sure your lease is in order. A good lease agreement sets out the rules landlords and tenants agree to comply with in their rental relationship. It is both a legal contract and a crucial document outlining the terms of the agreement including policies, restrictions, and the responsibilities of each party.

As a landlord, you are responsible for complying with federal, state, and local laws when it comes to the use and condition of the property. For example, you cannot discriminate against renters based on age, sex, religion, or ethnicity in compliance with the federal Fair Housing Act. Another act worthy of attention is the Uniform Residential Landlord and Tenant Act, which is used by many states to govern every aspect of residential tenancy. There are even laws requiring you to disclose to tenants any lead-based paint hazards, and on a local level, some areas have enacted laws regarding rent control that govern how much the rent may be increased at the end of any given lease term.

To find out which rental laws apply to your area, contact your state attorney general's office and local housing authorities to obtain information about local laws pertaining to tenants' rights. You can also consult your HOLD agent, property manager, or attorney who should be well-versed in the latest renditions of such laws. This is essential, as failure to understand and comply with legal restrictions could cost you dearly—monetarily and reputation-wise. For example, in Arizona, if you don't account for the tenant's deposit within the time allowed by law, you could be subject to pay them triple the amount.

Just as important as avoiding discrimination against protected classes, you should be aware of your rights as a property owner. For instance, many landlords don't like pets. Dogs and cats make lovely companions, but not everyone loves the wear and tear they can create on flooring, screen doors, and the lawn. Some dog breeds may even be prohibited by your insurer. Most require additional pet deposits and some refuse pets altogether. That's your choice. Additionally, you may want to limit the number of tenants or lean toward working professionals over undergrads from the local party college. For example, one landlord learned the hard way about renting to a trucker as he endured complaints for a year about the big rig being parked out front, which many neighbors considered an eyesore. Think through your decisions, ask what you can and can't do, and then be consistent. The worst thing you could do is reject five straight applicants because they were long-line truckers and then make an exception for your buddy, Pete, who drives a Peterbilt for a living. The five rejects may now be able to make a case that you discriminated against them illegally. It's serious stuff that could ruin your reputation and cause substantial financial and legal grief.

Put your leasing standards in writing and hand them out to all applicants. If you want to make any nontraditional exceptions or addendums to your lease, review them carefully with an attorney to make sure you indeed have those rights and the best way to execute them.

What should your lease contain?

You can obtain a copy of a standard, promulgated lease agreement that is applicable for your area online or from your HOLD team of experts. Lease forms, like all contracts, may be subject to negotiation. Both the landlord and the tenant have the right to change the terms and conditions of any preprinted lease.

These are some of the most important items to make sure and cover in your lease or rental agreement based on our experience.

- **Names**

  Include the names of all adult tenants who will occupy the rental property with signatures from each. This makes each tenant legally responsible for all terms of the agreement and enables you to legally seek the entire rent from any one of them should the others skip out or be unable to pay. Your agreement should clearly specify that the rental unit is the residence of only the tenants who have signed the lease and their minor children. This allows you to limit the number of occupants to those who have been approved and to evict a tenant who moves in a friend or relative, or sublets the unit without your permission.

- **Lease term**

  Every rental document should state whether it is a month-to-month or a fixed-term agreement. A month-to-month lease, which automatically renews unless terminated by you or the tenant, gives you more flexibility. You can end or modify a month-to-month lease or make changes any time you wish by giving the tenant notice (usually thirty days), which should be stated in the lease. When the lease is for a fixed term of six months, one year, or two years, neither you nor the tenant can end or modify the lease before the end of the term without the permission of the other. Fixed-term leases protect you from the unpredictability of tenant move-outs as long as the agreement is reinforced by adequate security deposits. You can of course list your repercussions and process for breaking the lease, as it will come up at some point with some tenant. We don't recommend granting a six-month lease because that causes you to deal with two vacancies in a year.

- **Rent**

  Specify the rent amount, when it is due (typically, the first of the month), acceptable payment methods (i.e., personal check, cashier's check, etc.), what late fees will be assessed if the rent is not paid on time, and any charges if a rent check bounces. It's important to check with your municipality and determine whether taxes are due on the rent; if so, be sure to add them to the lease.

- **Security deposit**

  State the dollar amount of the security deposit, how it may be used (cleaning, damage repair, etc.), how it may not be used (to pay the final month's rent), and when it will be returned at the end of the lease. It's also a good idea, and may in fact be a legal requirement where your property is located, to include details on where the security deposit is being held and whether interest on the deposit will be paid to the tenant.

- **Repairs and maintenance**

  Clearly set out your and the tenant's responsibilities for repairs and maintenance in your lease or rental agreement. This should include a requirement that the tenant alert you to defective or dangerous conditions in the rental property, restrictions on tenant repairs and alterations without your permission, and a condition that the tenant maintains the rental premises in clean and habitable condition and pays for any damage caused by abuse or neglect.

- **Right to enter property**

  To avoid tenant claims of illegal entry or violation of privacy rights, clarify your legal right of access to the property for repairs and inspections and how much advance notice you will provide.

- **Restrictions on illegal activity**

  To prevent property damage and limit your exposure to lawsuits, include an explicit clause prohibiting disruptive behavior, such as excessive noise, and illegal activity, such as drug dealing or operating a business where zoning ordinances prohibit it. It is also important if your property has a homeowners association that the lease requires the tenant to comply with any and all covenants or restrictions.

- **Pets**

  As discussed, be clear on whether you do or do not allow pets. If you do, identify any restrictions, such as a limit on the size or number of pets, as well as any added security deposits or monthly fees.

- **Renew, modify, terminate**

  Explain what happens at the end of the lease term, such as an option to renew, conversion of the lease to a lesser term, and/or requiring notice of termination by the tenant to the landlord.

- **Extras**

  Be sure your lease or rental agreement complies with all relevant laws including rent control ordinances, health and safety codes, occupancy rules, and antidiscrimination laws. State laws are especially critical, such as security deposit limits, notice requirements for entering the rental property, rules for changing or ending a tenancy, and specific disclosure requirements such as past flooding in the rental unit. Important rules and regulations covering parking and use of common areas should also be specifically mentioned in the lease agreement.

5. Sign the Lease and Collect Deposits

Once the application is approved, the lease can be prepared and signed by the new tenant and a move-in date scheduled. Notify the applicant and set up an appointment to sign. This will give you an opportunity to explain the lease contents and answer any questions the tenant may have.

If the application is not approved, notify the applicant of the denial, explain the reason, and follow up with an Application Denial Letter to keep for your records. Remember in this letter to always comply with the federal Fair Housing Act. Your HOLD attorney would again be a great resource for review.

Before you hand over a key, be sure to have the tenant sign the lease and then collect the money for the deposits (one typically charges a security deposit equal to one month's rent along with a nonrefundable cleaning deposit), the first month's rent, and any other fees or expenses required—pet expense, etc. All money should be in the form of a cashier's check or money order rather than a personal check—again, it is better record keeping for both you and your tenant. A good business practice is to never give occupancy unless you have received the cash or certified funds.

6. Move In

Before a tenant moves in, it's a good idea to inspect the property using the Move-In Walk-Through Inspection Form—found in Figure 12-8—to make sure that everything is clean, working, and in tenant-ready condition. Most inspections tend to be a formality. However, Jennice remembers one particular incident that was quite the opposite. A home they managed in Tempe, Arizona, had been rented to tenants who were moving from out of town. Move-in morning dawned and a property manager hurried over to do a last-minute inspection. Opening the door, she discovered a shocking sight: two pigeons had been trapped inside the home for a week. Everywhere she looked was a horrible mess. Fortunately, they were able to get a crew out to clean the property and get it back in shape before the tenants arrived. But imagine if they had waited until the tenants were already there!

At sign-up, present all your tenants with a New Tenant Information Packet containing their copy of the lease, a list of rules, telephone and email contacts, along with a copy of the property keys and any security codes and remotes. If the tenant will not be occupying the property within a few days, it may be better to schedule a time when they can obtain the keys for the property closer to the actual occupancy date.

Before you move anyone in, notify your mortgage company and the homeowners association, if applicable. Also be sure to call the utility companies to inform them a new occupant is moving in and to discontinue service under your account. This helps avoid having to collect utility costs incurred by the new tenant. When your tenant moves in, they are required to put the utilities in their name as of the effective date of their lease. The utility companies will send you a final bill.

You will also need to talk to your insurance agent about getting a "landlord type" policy on your property rather than a homeowner's policy. A landlords policy will give you the added coverage of rent loss if there is any damage to your property that prevents it from being rented while it is being repaired. You should also ask your tenants to get a renter's policy that will cover their belongings, so if any items are damaged by a

MOVE-IN WALK-THROUGH INSPECTION FORM

Move In: _____

Move Out: _____

Inspected By: _____

Key:
C = Clean, D = Dirty
1 - Needs Replaced, 2 - Needs Repaired,
3 - Slight Wear, 4 - Excellent

1. Kitchen

Doors/Locks	C D 1 2 3 4	
Walls/Ceiling	C D 1 2 3 4	
Floor	C D 1 2 3 4	
Stove	C D 1 2 3 4	
Stove Pans	C D 1 2 3 4	
Oven	C D 1 2 3 4	
Microwave	C D 1 2 3 4	
Countertop	C D 1 2 3 4	
Sink	C D 1 2 3 4	
Faucet	C D 1 2 3 4	
Dishwasher	C D 1 2 3 4	
Refrigerator	C D 1 2 3 4	
Blinds	C D 1 2 3 4	
Screens	C D 1 2 3 4	
Cabinets	C D 1 2 3 4	
Garbage Disposal	C D 1 2 3 4	
Vent Fan	C D 1 2 3 4	
Pantry	C D 1 2 3 4	

2. Dining Room

Walls/Ceiling	C D 1 2 3 4
Floor	C D 1 2 3 4
Blinds	C D 1 2 3 4
Screens	C D 1 2 3 4

3. Living Room

Walls/Ceiling	C D 1 2 3 4
Floor	C D 1 2 3 4
Blinds	C D 1 2 3 4
Screens	C D 1 2 3 4
Ceiling Fan	C D 1 2 3 4

4. Family Room

Walls/Ceiling	C D 1 2 3 4
Floor	C D 1 2 3 4
Blinds	C D 1 2 3 4
Screens	C D 1 2 3 4
Ceiling Fan	C D 1 2 3 4

5. Hall Baths

Doors/Locks	C D 1 2 3 4
Walls/Ceiling	C D 1 2 3 4
Floor	C D 1 2 3 4
Toilet	C D 1 2 3 4
Basin/Faucet	C D 1 2 3 4
Tub/Shower	C D 1 2 3 4
Blinds/Screen	C D 1 2 3 4
Medicine Cabinet	C D 1 2 3 4
Towel Bar	C D 1 2 3 4
Paper Holder	C D 1 2 3 4
Mirror	C D 1 2 3 4

6. Master Bedroom

Doors/Locks	C D 1 2 3 4
Walls/Ceiling	C D 1 2 3 4
Floor	C D 1 2 3 4
Closet	C D 1 2 3 4
Blinds	C D 1 2 3 4
Screens	C D 1 2 3 4
Ceiling Fan	C D 1 2 3 4

7. Master Bath

Doors/Locks	C D 1 2 3 4
Walls/Ceiling	C D 1 2 3 4
Floor	C D 1 2 3 4
Toilet	C D 1 2 3 4
Basin/Faucet	C D 1 2 3 4
Tub	C D 1 2 3 4
Shower	C D 1 2 3 4
Blinds/Screen	C D 1 2 3 4
Medicine Cabinet	C D 1 2 3 4
Towel Bar	C D 1 2 3 4
Paper Holder	C D 1 2 3 4
Mirror	C D 1 2 3 4

8. Fireplace

Grate/Screen	C D 1 2 3 4
Hearth/Mantle	C D 1 2 3 4

9. Additional Bedroom

Doors/Locks	C D 1 2 3 4
Walls/Ceiling	C D 1 2 3 4
Floor	C D 1 2 3 4
Closet	C D 1 2 3 4
Blinds	C D 1 2 3 4
Screens	C D 1 2 3 4
Ceiling Fan	C D 1 2 3 4

10. Additional Bedroom

Doors/Locks	C D 1 2 3 4
Walls/Ceiling	C D 1 2 3 4
Floor	C D 1 2 3 4
Closet	C D 1 2 3 4
Blinds	C D 1 2 3 4
Screens	C D 1 2 3 4
Ceiling Fan	C D 1 2 3 4

11. Additional Bedroom

Doors/Locks	C D 1 2 3 4
Walls/Ceiling	C D 1 2 3 4
Floor	C D 1 2 3 4
Closet	C D 1 2 3 4
Blinds	C D 1 2 3 4
Screens	C D 1 2 3 4
Ceiling Fan	C D 1 2 3 4

12. Additional Bedroom

Doors/Locks	C D 1 2 3 4
Walls/Ceiling	C D 1 2 3 4
Floor	C D 1 2 3 4
Closet	C D 1 2 3 4
Blinds	C D 1 2 3 4
Screens	C D 1 2 3 4
Ceiling Fan	C D 1 2 3 4

13. Den/Loft

Doors/Locks	C D 1 2 3 4
Walls/Ceiling	C D 1 2 3 4
Floor	C D 1 2 3 4
Blinds	C D 1 2 3 4
Screens	C D 1 2 3 4
Ceiling Fan	C D 1 2 3 4

14. Additional Bath

Doors/Locks	C D 1 2 3 4
Walls/Ceiling	C D 1 2 3 4
Floor	C D 1 2 3 4
Toilet	C D 1 2 3 4
Basin/Faucet	C D 1 2 3 4
Tub	C D 1 2 3 4
Shower	C D 1 2 3 4
Blinds/Screen	C D 1 2 3 4
Medicine Cabinet	C D 1 2 3 4
Towel Bar	C D 1 2 3 4
Paper Holder	C D 1 2 3 4
Mirror	C D 1 2 3 4

15. Hall

Coat Closet	C D 1 2 3 4
Linen Closet	C D 1 2 3 4
A/C Filter	C D 1 2 3 4
Smoke Detectors	C D 1 2 3 4

16. Utility Room

Doors/Locks	C D 1 2 3 4
Walls/Ceiling	C D 1 2 3 4
Floor	C D 1 2 3 4
Drapes/Blinds	C D 1 2 3 4
Screens	C D 1 2 3 4
Washer	C D 1 2 3 4
Dryer	C D 1 2 3 4

17. Garage

Doors/Locks	C D 1 2 3 4
Walls/Ceiling	C D 1 2 3 4
Floor	C D 1 2 3 4
Remotes	_____

18. Exterior Condition

Paint/Trim	C D 1 2 3 4
Roofing	C D 1 2 3 4
Patio Lights	C D 1 2 3 4
Patio	C D 1 2 3 4
Fence/Gates	C D 1 2 3 4
Landscape Front	1 2 3 4
Landscape Back	1 2 3 4
Doorbell	C D 1 2 3 4

19. Other Items

Pool	C D 1 2 3 4
Spa	C D 1 2 3 4
RO	1 2 3 4
Barbecue	C D 1 2 3 4

Notes:

Figure 12-8

Available for download at www.KellerINK.com.

fire or flood, your insurance is not responsible. We state in the tenant's lease that they need to get renters insurance. Although there is no way to require them to get coverage, we highly suggest that they do so.

Renting your investment property is a huge milestone on your journey. You now have more than an expectation of monthly cash flow, and you have a legally binding lease agreement that guarantees it for the duration of the lease. Pop the bubbly. Your investment adventure has left the tarmac and has officially taken flight!

This is when many investors return they focus to lead generating for their next acquisition and aggressively saving capital to afford it. It's also a period of time when you can make systematic improvements to your properties and investment business to increase the value of your holdings. But that's for the next chapter.

POINTS TO REMEMBER

- Promote. Effective targeted marketing—including yard signs, ads in community and city newspapers and online advertising, fliers and brochures—will drive interest in your property and provide a larger pool of prospective tenants from which to choose. For the widest reach, you may consider listing your property with a real estate agent and utilizing their resources.

- Before you put your property on the rental market, contact your HOLD team and ask them to do a CMA, or Comparative Market Analysis. You may consider lowering the rent by a small amount to attract a wider range of prospects and avoid vacancy.

- Screen the tenant before leasing. Take the time to meet potential tenants in person and run a credit, employment, and rental history check before agreeing to rent to someone. Calculate their rent-to-income ratio by dividing the rent for the property by their verified monthly income. An acceptable ratio is considered to be less than 33 percent.

- Be sure your lease agreement complies with federal, state, and local laws governing rental property.

- Before you move in the new tenant, notify your mortgage company, homeowners association, and utility companies to inform them that tenants are moving in and have them discontinue your service.

- Obtain landlords insurance to protect you from property damage, liability, and loss of rent.

CHAPTER 13: INCREASE VALUE

✓ **3. BUY**
An investment property where you make money going in

Outcome: a profitable property to add to your HOLD investment portfolio

↓

4. MANAGE
Your tenants and properties like a pro

☑ **Chapter 12**: Find Good Tenants

☐ **Chapter 13**: Increase Value

☐ **Chapter 14**: Run It Like a Business

Outcome: a sustainable investment property for your HOLD portfolio

After reading this chapter, you will know how to:

☐ Manage your finances.

☐ Manage maintenance and repairs.

☐ Manage your tenants.

VALUE YOUR PROPERTY AND TENANTS

A rental property is a great investment, but your duties don't stop once you sign a renter and move them in. As we've said, managing a rental property is just like running any other business, and you need to be purposeful, accurate, and knowledgeable in three key areas to successfully manage your property and increase value: 1. Manage Your Finances, 2. Manage Maintenance and Repairs, and 3. Manage Your Tenants.

Yes, there will be paperwork, billing, customer service, and vendor relations, but there will also be cash flow, equity buildup, and tax benefits. There are two kinds of investments—passive and active. Most people are familiar with the former and less so with the later. Passive ownership is like picking stocks or mutual funds; you have to engage at the point of purchase and make the best possible selection, but your responsibility largely ends there. You're banking on the leadership of the companies or funds you invest in to manage that investment to higher returns in the future. Other than occasionally rebalancing your portfolio, you've entrusted your wealth building to others. Active ownership, like your HOLD property, works differently. You are the person who will be most responsible for the overall long-term success of this investment. Even if you seek the help of a property manager, you'll still have to make critical decisions about tenants, weigh the costs of improvements today vs. repairs tomorrow, establish and maintain records and, all the while, keep a keen eye on the bottom line. It seems like a tall order but it's quite manageable with the right systems in place. And, better yet, it's financially rewarding. The yield on active investments is almost always higher than passive. When you invest your time in addition to your money, it seems only reasonable that there's a financial incentive.

In this chapter, we will deal with the nuts and bolts of managing your rental property and tenants. We'll share the forms and processes that work for us, show you how to set up your accounting, select vendors, handle noncompliance issues, evictions, lease renewals, move-outs, and more. We'll even help you decide when it's appropriate to seek the help of a property manager.

For your property on 742 Evergreen Terrace you've collected rent and deposits, but where do you deposit them? Can you simply deposit everything in your checking account and keep track or is more required? All these questions and more are why the next step after renting your property is to get your finances in order for your investment business.

1. MANAGE YOUR FINANCES

While you don't need to become certified as a public accountant to manage your rental property finances, you will likely need to learn some basic accounting. We believe in the idea of thinking big. It's far better to model your start-up investment business after a large established one than to simple "wing it" and make corrections as you go. First, it doesn't require substantially more work in the beginning and, second, you'll never have to reinvent or overhaul your systems. Because they are based on the same fundamental systems as big firms, you'll simply scale them up to match the size of your investment portfolio. The HOLD system for financial management is relatively simple and should serve you well, no matter how far you take your investment career.

In our experience, there are two types of accounting you will be responsible for as your own property manager, and we suggest opening two bank accounts to help you manage them. The primary account, or business checking account, will be where you deposit the monthly budget—i.e., the monthly expenses, for your single-family home on Evergreen Terrace. This will allow you to run the business and pay all budgeted expenses each month. The second account will be a depository one where you store all of your remaining rental income, or your net operating income. This will be an interest-bearing account so that you can continue to make money on your cash flow. Bear in mind, you may need a third account for deposit checks. In many areas, you'll be required to keep that money separate or in a trust account. Ask your CPA for advice.

Most large or regional banks offer packages for small businesses. After the initial setup, the additional accounts cost little (or are free) and you can move money freely between them online. Tip: As your investment portfolio grows, label your different checkbooks clearly. If all your checks are generic blue, it's easy to grab the wrong one when you're racing to the property to meet the landscapers. And at the end of the month, you'll be scratching your head trying to balance your accounts. A Sharpie or a label machine can prevent that from ever happening.

Initially, your accounting needs will be fairly simple. There are a number of quality property management software packages that perform integrated accounting and property management reporting functions. The price for this software is usually around $200 for something like QuickBooks. Or you could do like many investors and simply use an Excel spreadsheet. If you start with Excel or another free solution, make sure you're tracking your financials in a way that will easily translate to exporting them into a professional solution like QuickBooks later. To help keep things straight, track your expenses and income in three different categories: your accounts payable, your accounts receivable, and your miscellaneous accounts. Accounts payable is a fancy way of saying expenses. These will be all the regular bills you pay. Accounts receivable? You guessed it, that's your income. The miscellaneous category is a catch-all for expenses and income that don't occur on a regular basis (like late fees from bounced check charges).

Accounts Payable

One of the things you will need to decide is how often you will pay bills: once a week, twice a month, or monthly. Whichever payment cycle you choose, there may be some exceptions due to unique vendor payment requirements.

There are basically two ways you can set up your bill pay—monthly or recurring. Monthly bills are accompanied by an actual statement or invoice each month, such as utilities and other services. Recurring bills are automatically paid each month on a set schedule, such as insurance. Invoices are typically not associated with these bills or are sent electronically.

Whether the payment is monthly or recurring is up to you, as most bills give you a choice. Either way, the first thing you must do is set up an account for vendors in your accounting program, or a consistent label in your Excel spreadsheet (like "Crazy Aaron Lawn Service") so that you can sort transactions related to these vendors quickly and easily.

When a monthly bill or invoice is received, verify the amount, pay it, mail it, and post it in your books. For recurring bills, refer to the list of vendors you've already set up and enter their payments according to the predetermined schedule.

Accounts Receivable

All money you collect on the property is considered accounts receivable. As we suggested earlier, the excess money after monthly expenses—or your net operating income—should be deposited in your interest-bearing depository account. Keep in mind, there may be other funds appropriate for this account aside from rental income. This includes refunds such as utility deposits, escrow excess, and insurance reimbursements. Some others might be late fees incurred by your tenant and taxes. Just make sure to keep all income other than expenses in this account, which will be a great place to save up your next property's down payment.

Miscellaneous Accounts

As previously mentioned, there will be other accounting functions besides accounts payable and accounts receivable for which your property management business will be responsible. Insufficient fund issues and bank account reconciliation are examples of these.

As with most of life's unexpected surprises, it is important to be prepared so that you can deal with such circumstances quickly. For instance, there are several things you can do when you receive a check with insufficient funds, and you will need to decide which policy best fits your business. A few suggestions in this case are:

- Charge a fee.

- Redeposit the check.

- Notify the tenant and request a cashier's check.

- Serve the tenant with a five-day notice.

- All of the above.

Regardless of your strategy here, make sure that once you come to a decision, you put it in writing and stick with it across the board—with all properties and all tenants. The last thing you want is one tenant catching wind of a leniency he wasn't afforded.

During this period when you're setting up accounts, many investors naturally ask the question whether or not to set up a corporation. There are whole books written on the topic and, frankly, this is a conversation for you, your CPA, and possibly your attorney. The costs and protections provided by various corporate entities vary widely and can be customized to your needs. One of the reasons we advised you to consider an umbrella insurance policy is because it can afford you great protection while you weigh your options on investing in setting up an entity. The primary exception to that rule would be if you are working with partners. One thing an entity will do that insurance won't is shield you from the liability of one of your partners making a legal or financial mistake. At the very least, this is a great time to start that conversation with your HOLD advisers.

Lastly, as a matter of good practice, time block to reconcile your bank accounts each month upon receiving your bank statements. In fact, when you're first starting out, it's not a bad idea to pick a time once a week to review your financials and make sure everything is up to date and in order. Monthly check-ins are the standard, as many bills will need to be paid on this schedule. However, finding time for quick review more frequently is never a bad thing. And, the more often you do it and on a regular basis, it will become habit and no longer seem daunting. As your profit grows, we'll bet you start enjoying this time block to look at your wealth-building journey and pat yourself on the back for your accomplishments.

For example, let's say the numbers we used in the Analyze section for 742 Evergreen Terrace proved correct in year one. At the end of the year, you would realize an annual cash flow of about $800, appreciation of about $6,600, and debt pay down of more than $1,000 for a total return on investment of about 19 percent. By year fifteen, those numbers will have increased to an annual cash flow of over $6,000—for an accumulated cash flow of nearly $49,000—an appreciation of about $12,000—an accumulated appreciation of more than $136,000, and a total debt pay down of over $26,000, for a total return on investment of 47 percent. While these projections are purely hypothetical, they are based on reasonable assumptions and are the kind of results investors enjoy when they manage their properties, especially their finances, well over time.

Doesn't sound like such a bad way to spend a Sunday morning after all. And to help you get to that level of success, figure 13-1 will give you a starter's checklist when it comes to investor accounting.

Initial Accounting Setup Checklist

☐ Meet with a reputable CPA. It should be your goal to find one who is knowledgeable in this type of business. (You don't want to be the guinea pig.)

☐ Start the conversation with your HOLD advisers about the pros and cons of setting up a corporate entity to hold your property.

☐ Open up your primary and depository bank accounts.

☐ If necessary, establish a separate or trust account for your security deposits as well. This should be an interest-bearing account. The money you receive for security deposits has to be held until the end of the lease. Some states require that you pay interest to the tenant. If you combine the security deposits for all of your tenants, you may still be able to make more interest than the state requires you to pay the tenant.

☐ Buy and install accounting software to track and pay company expenses. Or work with your CPA to set up and track expenses via a spreadsheet.

☐ If your accounting software doesn't come with one, ask your CPA about establishing a "chart of accounts" for you recordkeeping. A chart of accounts predefines categories for expenses and income so that you can track them according to industry norms. The labels change from business to business so you will want one for property management.

☐ Have your CPA review your setup.

☐ If applicable, have your CPA meet and train you or your bookkeeper as to how they want the bookkeeping handled.

Figure 13-1

2. MANAGE MAINTENANCE AND REPAIRS

Once your financials and related procedures are squared away, it's important to enact strategies around property maintenance and repairs. We suggest preparing for the worst, the unexpected—everything that "could" happen.

That way you won't lose time or money debating how to solve the problem. The flowchart in figure 13-2 shows what we consider the main steps to follow, from request to completion, for property maintenance and repairs.

With your finance systems squared away, it's time to get a plan for property maintenance and repairs. Houses are fairly complex when you think about it. Besides the component parts—foundation, walls, roof, and landscape—that provide shelter and structure, every home includes complex systems for ventilation, heating and cooling, electricity, plumbing, insulation, and the list goes on. Even the dedicated do-it-yourselfer will want to build a rolodex of reliable contractors to do general or specialized work when they can't themselves because of lack of time, desire or skill. There is nothing wrong with building sweat equity by installing new laminate floors or touching up the paint one weekend, but you need to plan in advance for where you will draw the line. Make the decision ahead of time for when to grab your toolbox and when to reach for the phone.

In the Analyze portion we budgeted $66 a month (or $792 a year) for maintenance and repairs. The idea is that most months you will have neither and can slowly accumulate enough money to cover a big-ticket item, like a failing HVAC system. By beginning with a financial plan for repairs, you're ahead of the game. Now you just need a game plan for executing smart and timely maintenance and being responsive when your tenant calls and needs a repairman. The following flowchart in figure 13-2 shows what many consider the main steps to follow, from request to completion, for repairs.

As a landlord, you are responsible for maintaining your rental property and making it safe and habitable for your tenants. Some states have laws governing how landlords must keep up their rental properties, while

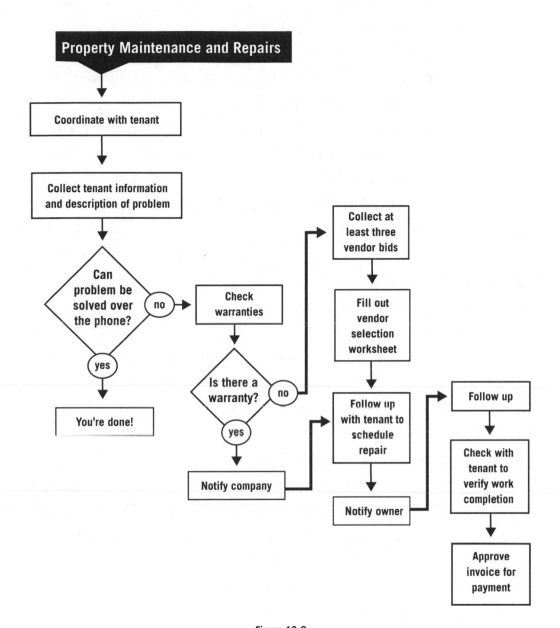

Figure 13-2

others leave it up to your good judgment. Regardless of what the law says, proper upkeep of your property is just good business. While this will certainly make your tenants happy and attract high quality ones, it's also about protecting your investment.

With proper preventive maintenance, your property should remain in good condition and not require excessive repairs. It is a good idea to make plans ahead of time to deal with any necessary repairs or maintenance problems that will arise as a matter of course throughout the life of a property.

Choosing a Vendor

One of the biggest stumbling blocks for many would-be landlords is the tenant's call in the middle of the night with a maintenance disaster. For all of us but the most dedicated handymen, that call doesn't mean that we crawl out of bed and grab a plunger or a wrench and speed off through the night. It just means that after we take down the information and hang up, we hit the speed dial for our go-to plumber.

Assembling a list of skilled, reliable service providers and finding a good general handyman will save you from those dreaded phone calls and help preserve your property—and sanity. We work off referrals, talking to real estate agents, other investors, and property managers to get the names of resources they use and trust. One of the hardest to find is the general handyman. We'll find someone who is qualified and priced right—then, six months later, they're a general contractor and won't take jobs less than $10,000. We're constantly looking for skilled repair people and you should learn to do this as well. Ask your HOLD investor network, friends, family, even your kid's teachers. If you keep it top of mind, you'll be amazed how many great vendors you'll find just through word of mouth.

Even though we rely heavily on our trusted network, whenever we get a good lead, we still make it a point to schedule an interview with all prospective vendors. We want to know exactly what services they provide, if they're licensed, their rates, references, example jobs, etc. To help you with the interview process, figure 13-3 provides a great way to track and consolidate all of your various vendor needs mentioned above.

Maintenance and Repair Worksheet			
Question	Vendor #1	Vendor #2	Vendor #3
What services do they provide?	__ roofing __ painting __ carpentry __ plumbing __ electrical __ landscaping __ pool/spa __ other _____	__ roofing __ painting __ carpentry __ plumbing __ electrical __ landscaping __ pool/spa __ other _____	__ roofing __ painting __ carpentry __ plumbing __ electrical __ landscaping __ pool/spa __ other _____
What are their rates? Do they have a minimum charge?			
Do they have workmen's compensation insurance?	Yes / No	Yes / No	Yes / No
Is there a trip charge? What is it?	Yes / No	Yes / No	Yes / No
Do they support emergency calls?	Yes / No	Yes / No	Yes / No
What are their off-hour charges?			
Contact person:			
Billing address:			
Phone number: After hours number:			
Notes:			

Figure 13-3

Even if you have a specific vendor you like, don't discount other recommendations you receive. Rather, benchmark them against each other to make sure you're getting the most efficient service for the best price. Look at figure 13-4 for an example in the cleaning industry.

Vendor Selection Worksheet

Question	Vendor #1	Vendor #2	Vendor #3
What is the base charge? What does this include?	Cost $ _____ ___bathrooms ___windows / screens ___window treatments ___carpets ___floors ___oven / refrigerator ___walls ___other _____	Cost $ _____ ___bathrooms ___windows / screens ___window treatments ___carpets ___floors ___oven / refrigerator ___walls ___other _____	Cost $ _____ ___bathrooms ___windows / screens ___window treatments ___carpets ___floors ___oven / refrigerator ___walls ___other _____
Contact person:			
Billing address:			
Phone number: After-hours number:			
Notes:			

Figure 13-4

Having your trusted team of vendors in place will set you at ease in case something does go wrong in the unforeseeable future. It will also help you get necessary work done in a timely and cost-effective manner.

Maintenance

Preventive maintenance and upkeep of your property can mean something as small as keeping the lawn mowed and the HVAC filters changed, or as substantial as repainting the property or paying for a new roof.

In most areas, it's fairly common for the tenants to be responsible for basic upkeep, especially things like watering and mowing the lawn or replacing air filters. Some tenants will offer to do more in exchange for lower rent and this can be a cheap way to handle things if they have the skills. Just make sure you clearly define the tenants' maintenance duties in the lease agreement terms.

For more advanced tasks, like servicing a HVAC system, you'll want to hire a specialist. Many times you can handle these between tenants. We know some investors who have their properties inspected every 5 to 6 years (just like when they did their pre-close due diligence) to ensure they know the current state of the property.

Some items have a natural lifespan and you can predict and budget when these replacement costs will hit. The National Association of Home Builders / Bank of America conducted a comprehensive telephone survey of manufacturers, trade associations, and researchers to develop information about the longevity of housing components. How long each component will last depends on the quality of installation, maintenance, weather, and climate conditions and the intensity of use, but figure 13-5 provides a general guideline for typical home components and systems.

Life Expectancy of Home Components	
Component/System	**Life Span**
Roof	15–20 years
Siding	30–40 years
Furnace	20–30 years
Plumbing	40–50 years
Air Conditioner (central)	10–15 years
Major Appliances (washer/dryer, refrigerator, range)	12–15 years

Figure 13-5

But before you can do the work, you'll need the right vendor for each job. As a general rule, maintenance is a pay-me-now or pay-me-later scenario. Landlords that ignore aging systems or always go for the cheapest solution will often pay the price later when systems break down for good. You don't need to gold plate your investment property, but you do want to give it some genuine TLC and make regular investments in the maintenance of the structure and systems.

Repairs

If something breaks, malfunctions, or becomes inoperable, it is the responsibility of the landlord to repair it as quickly as possible. Normally, a landlord is required to provide repair when the damage is not the fault of the tenant, such as a toilet seal breaking and causing the tank to overflow. Even if the damage is the tenant's fault, you will still need to repair it—especially if it concerns the so-called necessities of daily life, such as running water, heat, air-conditioning, and proper ventilation. That being said, you can bill a tenant for any repairs that can be shown are the result of their actions.

When the tenant calls to report a problem or needed repair, determine first if it can be fixed over the phone. If so, you're done! Otherwise, a vendor will need to be notified to inspect, estimate, and complete the repair.

Collect the tenant information (name, address, phone number), their availability, and a way to reach them and give it directly to the vendor. Let your tenant know that a vendor will be contacting them to set up an appointment to make the necessary repairs.

Once you have a handle on what the repair is, you can ask your vendor to let you know an estimate cost. There may be payment options that need to be considered before calling for repair, including home warranties, builder warranties, or appliance warranties. If these exist for the reported problem, you will need to notify the company directly to get directions for completing the repair. Failure to do this may result in nonpayment from the company. If no warranty is available, order the repair using one of your preapproved vendors.

As far as scheduling the actual repair, it's much easier to let the tenant and vendor make arrangements according to their calendars. This way you don't have to play middle man in making their schedules work, and your tenant takes responsibility for getting the problem fixed in a timetable that works for them.

Once the repair is completed, either inspect it yourself or follow up with the tenant to ensure that the repair was completed and is acceptable. If not, notify the vendor for resolution. If the repair was acceptable, the invoice can be approved for payment. Remember, a well-maintained home is more likely to increase in value, attract better tenants, charge higher rents, and in the end will cost you less to maintain than one that is continually duct-taped together. There is no economic value in delaying a repair. You're going to have to do it eventually, and if you wait, not only will the problem have gotten worse (and, possibly, more expensive), but you will also have alienated your client: the tenant. Which brings us to our next big management topic ... managing your renters.

3. MANAGE YOUR TENANTS

Now that you've found the right tenants, take care of them. By that we mean create a relationship based on mutual respect and courtesy. Return phone calls promptly, be responsible with repairs, and communicate clearly and openly. Surprises can lead to misunderstandings, and misunderstandings can lead to conflict. Remember, you control one of the most important elements in the lives of your tenants: their home. If you treat them and "their home" with respect, they're much more likely to treat you and your property the same way.

There are many facets to a landlord/tenant relationship. Some are more challenging than others. The goal is to manage these relationships well and consistently. In the following sections, we'll share our systems for doing just that. A good system removes the guesswork. It allows you to act quickly and confidently and avoid unnecessary drama.

Lease Renewal

Before the end of a tenant's lease, you will need to decide whether or not to renew and what, if any, changes to rental rates or lease terms you want to make. Figure 13-6 represents how to think about this decision and its outcomes at the most basic level.

If	Then
You do not want to renew the lease and want to re-rent the property	Send the tenant a certified, written notice thirty days prior to the lease expiration, informing them that the lease will not be renewed and what the move-out date is.
You want to renew the lease	Send a renewal addendum to the tenants forty-five days prior to the expiration date.

Figure 13-6

As we discussed in chapter 12, your lease agreement terms should allow you to choose either of these options up front. It should also give the tenant the right to pursue both options and negotiate in either circumstance. That being said, if you decide to offer a lease renewal, you'll want to prepare a renewal addendum with any changes or modifications and the new lease expiration date. Send the addendum and a cover letter to the tenants approximately forty-five days prior to the lease expiration to give them some time to think it over and reply within the thirty-day notice period. If the tenant chooses to renew, you're pretty much set, and can continue your relationship recognizing any new prices or terms.

On the other hand, if you or the tenants choose not to renew the lease, you'll need to obtain signatures on the addendum, send a fully signed copy to the tenants, file the original, and follow the move-out procedures outlined in figure 13-7.

As soon as the tenant's notice is received and the move-out date is set, we send the tenant a notice confirming the information, along with

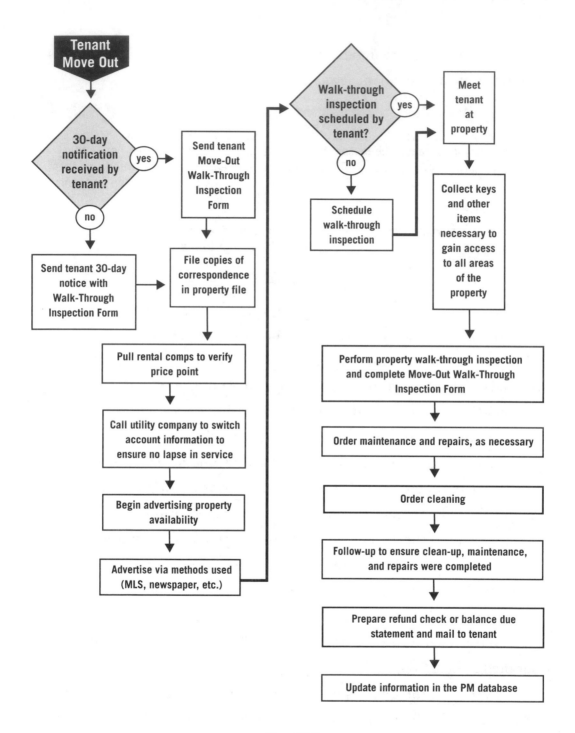

Figure 13-7

a Move-Out Walk-Through Inspection Form to let them know how the property will be inspected. Then we immediately turn our focus to advertising the property in hopes of keeping vacancy rates to a minimum.

- **Promote your property**

  As soon as you are aware of the date that the property will be vacant, you can begin to advertise its availability. At a minimum, you should place a sign in the yard to inform people of the property's availability for rent and how they can find out more information. To further advertise availability, use one or more of the techniques discussed in chapter 12.

- **Complete a walk-through inspection**

  The notice sent upon signing of a nonrenewal should be sent certified (receipt requested) to ensure and document that the tenant received the notice. Include a document similar to the one in figure 13-9 to let the tenant know exactly what will be looked at upon final walk-through. File copies of the notices, letters, and any other correspondence in the property file, making sure to indicate the date each was received. Then call the utility companies to switch account information to ensure no lapse in service, giving them the date you want to turn on service under your account.

  Perform the property inspection room by room using the Move-Out Walk-Through Inspection Form, or something similar that you have previously shared with the tenant. Remember, when the tenants first moved in, you completed an identical inspection form (see figure 12-8 on p. 199). Just like when you rent a car, the before and after comparison should be pretty easy. Any tenant-caused damage to the property should be noted on the inspection sheet so that repair costs can be properly deducted from the tenants' security deposit and the required work be done to get the house ready to re-rent. Be sure to test all the faucets, appliances, sprinklers, ceiling fans, and drawers, and note anything that is not working correctly.

The tenant moving out may or may not want to be present during the final walk-through inspection. Using simple if-then statements, figure 13-8 depicts best practices for each decision.

If	Then
The tenant does not want to be present for the inspection	Schedule the walk-through and collect the keys from the tenant. Once the tenant returns the keys, the inspection should be completed no later than the next day. As long as the tenant has possession of the keys, they are considered to be in possession of the property and can be charged rent.
The tenants wants to be present for the inspection	The tenant will schedule the walk-through inspection. Meet the tenant at the property at the specified time, and collect all keys and other items in possession that allows access to areas of the property at this time.

Figure 13-8

- **Order necessary maintenance and repairs**

  Routine maintenance and cleaning must be scheduled for as soon as a tenant has moved out of a property, along with specific maintenance and repairs that were noted in the walk-through inspection. Compare the walk-through sheet with the inspection report done by the tenant upon move-in to make sure that the individual is not charged for damage they did not do. Schedule the date and time for the cleaning

MOVE-OUT WALK-THROUGH INSPECTION FORM

Move In: _____

Move Out: _____

Inspected By: _____

Key:
C = Clean, D = Dirty
1 - Needs Replaced, 2 - Needs Repaired,
3 - Slight Wear, 4 - Excellent

1. Kitchen

Doors/Locks	C	D	1	2	3 4
Walls/Ceiling	C	D	1	2	3 4
Floor	C	D	1	2	3 4
Stove	C	D	1	2	3 4
Stove Pans	C	D	1	2	3 4
Oven	C	D	1	2	3 4
Microwave	C	D	1	2	3 4
Countertop	C	D	1	2	3 4
Sink	C	D	1	2	3 4
Faucet	C	D	1	2	3 4
Dishwasher	C	D	1	2	3 4
Refrigerator	C	D	1	2	3 4
Blinds	C	D	1	2	3 4
Screens	C	D	1	2	3 4
Cabinets	C	D	1	2	3 4
Garbage Disposal	C	D	1	2	3 4
Vent Fan	C	D	1	2	3 4
Pantry	C	D	1	2	3 4

2. Dining Room

Walls/Ceiling	C	D	1	2	3 4
Floor	C	D	1	2	3 4
Blinds	C	D	1	2	3 4
Screens	C	D	1	2	3 4

3. Living Room

Walls/Ceiling	C	D	1	2	3 4
Floor	C	D	1	2	3 4
Blinds	C	D	1	2	3 4
Screens	C	D	1	2	3 4
Ceiling Fan	C	D	1	2	3 4

4. Family Room

Walls/Ceiling	C	D	1	2	3 4
Floor	C	D	1	2	3 4
Blinds	C	D	1	2	3 4
Screens	C	D	1	2	3 4
Ceiling Fan	C	D	1	2	3 4

5. Hall Baths

Doors/Locks	C	D	1	2	3 4
Walls/Ceiling	C	D	1	2	3 4
Floor	C	D	1	2	3 4
Toilet	C	D	1	2	3 4
Basin/Faucet	C	D	1	2	3 4
Tub/Shower	C	D	1	2	3 4
Blinds/Screen	C	D	1	2	3 4
Medicine Cabinet	C	D	1	2	3 4
Towel Bar	C	D	1	2	3 4
Paper Holder	C	D	1	2	3 4
Mirror	C	D	1	2	3 4

6. Master Bedroom

Doors/Locks	C	D	1	2	3 4
Walls/Ceiling	C	D	1	2	3 4
Floor	C	D	1	2	3 4
Closet	C	D	1	2	3 4
Blinds	C	D	1	2	3 4
Screens	C	D	1	2	3 4
Ceiling Fan	C	D	1	2	3 4

7. Master Bath

Doors/Locks	C	D	1	2	3 4
Walls/Ceiling	C	D	1	2	3 4
Floor	C	D	1	2	3 4
Toilet	C	D	1	2	3 4
Basin/Faucet	C	D	1	2	3 4
Tub	C	D	1	2	3 4
Shower	C	D	1	2	3 4
Blinds/Screen	C	D	1	2	3 4
Medicine Cabinet	C	D	1	2	3 4
Towel Bar	C	D	1	2	3 4
Paper Holder	C	D	1	2	3 4
Mirror	C	D	1	2	3 4

8. Fireplace

Grate/Screen	C	D	1	2	3 4
Hearth/Mantle	C	D	1	2	3 4

9. Additional Bedroom

Doors/Locks	C	D	1	2	3 4
Walls/Ceiling	C	D	1	2	3 4
Floor	C	D	1	2	3 4
Closet	C	D	1	2	3 4
Blinds	C	D	1	2	3 4
Screens	C	D	1	2	3 4
Ceiling Fan	C	D	1	2	3 4

10. Additional Bedroom

Doors/Locks	C	D	1	2	3 4
Walls/Ceiling	C	D	1	2	3 4
Floor	C	D	1	2	3 4
Closet	C	D	1	2	3 4
Blinds	C	D	1	2	3 4
Screens	C	D	1	2	3 4
Ceiling Fan	C	D	1	2	3 4

11. Additional Bedroom

Doors/Locks	C	D	1	2	3 4
Walls/Ceiling	C	D	1	2	3 4
Floor	C	D	1	2	3 4
Closet	C	D	1	2	3 4
Blinds	C	D	1	2	3 4
Screens	C	D	1	2	3 4
Ceiling Fan	C	D	1	2	3 4

12. Additional Bedroom

Doors/Locks	C	D	1	2	3 4
Walls/Ceiling	C	D	1	2	3 4
Floor	C	D	1	2	3 4
Closet	C	D	1	2	3 4
Blinds	C	D	1	2	3 4
Screens	C	D	1	2	3 4
Ceiling Fan	C	D	1	2	3 4

13. Den/Loft

Doors/Locks	C	D	1	2	3
Walls/Ceiling	C	D	1	2	3
Floor	C	D	1	2	3
Blinds	C	D	1	2	3
Screens	C	D	1	2	3
Ceiling Fan	C	D	1	2	3

14. Additional Bath

Doors/Locks	C	D	1	2	3
Walls/Ceiling	C	D	1	2	3
Floor	C	D	1	2	3
Toilet	C	D	1	2	3
Basin/Faucet	C	D	1	2	3
Tub	C	D	1	2	3
Shower	C	D	1	2	3
Blinds/Screen	C	D	1	2	3
Medicine Cabinet	C	D	1	2	3
Towel Bar	C	D	1	2	3
Paper Holder	C	D	1	2	3
Mirror	C	D	1	2	3

15. Hall

Coat Closet	C	D	1	2	3
Linen Closet	C	D	1	2	3
A/C Filter	C	D	1	2	3
Smoke Detectors	C	D	1	2	3

16. Utility Room

Doors/Locks	C	D	1	2	3
Walls/Ceiling	C	D	1	2	3
Floor	C	D	1	2	3
Drapes/Blinds	C	D	1	2	3
Screens	C	D	1	2	3
Washer	C	D	1	2	3
Dryer	C	D	1	2	3

17. Garage

Doors/Locks	C	D	1	2	3
Walls/Ceiling	C	D	1	2	3
Floor	C	D	1	2	3
Remotes					_____

18. Exterior Condition

Paint/Trim	C	D	1	2	3
Roofing	C	D	1	2	3
Patio Lights	C	D	1	2	3
Patio	C	D	1	2	3
Fence/Gates	C	D	1	2	3
Landscape Front			1	2	3
Landscape Back			1	2	3
Doorbell	C	D	1	2	3

19. Other Items

Pool	C	D	1	2	3
Spa	C	D	1	2	3
RO			1	2	3
Barbecue	C	D	1	2	3

Notes:

Figure 13-9

Available for download at www.KellerINK.com.

crew. You can schedule this cleaning once you are aware of the property inspection date. You may also set up landscaping and pool services or arrange for a time you can do such duties to make the apartment move-in ready.

The tenant may choose to complete any necessary repairs that were identified during the inspection. If they ask you to take care of them, you will need to coordinate with the vendor and ensure that individual has access to the property when necessary. Scheduling and completing all maintenance and repairs in a timely manner is very important, not only to ensure that the property is ready to lease again, but also to calculate the security deposit refund within the time limits allowed by law.

Follow up to ensure that all work is completed and satisfactory once the vendors have notified you the maintenance and/or repairs have been completed. The property should now be ready to show and lease to prospective tenants.

- **Prepare the security deposit refund**

  Because the law dictates the time requirements for submitting security deposit refunds to tenants, preparing the security deposit refund must be done in a timely fashion. Make sure to check with the real estate laws for your state/area to identify special time requirements in this arena. Calculate the tenant security deposit refund, prepare the refund check made out to the tenant—or the balance due statement if additional money is owed—and mail it to them. We suggest certified return receipt mail for your records and assurance.

Tenant Notices

After reviewing the nonrenewal procedure, you may be wondering what happens if there are complications or varying opinions prior to the end of the lease. We're here to say that, unfortunately, there might be times when delinquent or noncompliance forms will need to be sent to tenants. This is not a fun experience by any means, but there are times when it is a necessary process. We're going to give you a high-level explanation of three specific legal notices you hopefully will never have to use: I. delinquent rent notice, II. noncompliance notice, and III. eviction notice.

I. Delinquent rent notice

A delinquent rent notice is sent to tenants who have not paid the rent on time according to the delinquency policy set out in your lease. Once a tenant is considered delinquent, send them a notice giving them a specified time period to pay the rent defined in your delinquent rental policy, typically within five days. The notice should either be mailed certified, return receipt or using a process server. If the notice is sent by mail, the time period should not begin until the receipt acknowledging that the tenant received the notice is returned to your office. At this point, you have two possible outcomes, which are outlined in figure 13-10.

If	Then
The tenant pays the rent within the time period stated on the notice	Assess the late fees, prepare the bill, and submit to the tenant.
The tenant does not pay the rent within the allowed time period stated on the notice	Begin the eviction procedure. (see eviction notice procedure)

Figure 13-10

II. Noncompliance notice

A noncompliance notice should be sent to the tenant anytime there has been a breach in the lease based on the noncompliance policy you established for your properties. This can be anything from an unauthorized pet or roommate to outright illegal activities. In most instances where your tenants aren't behaving as well as they should, a simple call can get them back on the straight and narrow. Just make note of it in your property file in case they fail to keep their word. When you send a noncompliance notice, you're really setting the stage for eviction. This is part of your paper trail to demonstrate that you gave the tenant full notice and, when appropriate, and opportunity to resolve the problem on their own.

In the event that you have to give them formal notice, send it to the tenant via certified, return receipt mail. Place a copy of the notice in the property file. Schedule an inspection with the tenant, following the allowed time period, to confirm that the required changes were made. Again, figure 13-11 offers your outcomes.

If	Then
The tenant is in compliance with the lease following the inspection	Document the findings of the inspection and place in the property file.
The tenant is not in compliance	Begin the eviction procedure. (see eviction notice procedure)

Figure 13-11

It's never pleasant, but once in a while, if a tenant doesn't pay their rent or fails to comply with the terms of the lease, you realize you will have to evict them. So what are the steps to evicting a tenant?

First of all, you will want to research the laws that are specific to your state. If you don't follow the steps precisely, you can lose the case in court or take weeks or even months to evict the tenant from your property.

Once you've established the local and state laws, try to talk to the tenant and find out why they are not in compliance. If you can't get the tenant to return your calls or meet with you, you can lock them out. In order to do this, you must have a key available for them within two hours at any time of the day or night, whether or not the issue is settled. Locking out a tenant is an extreme step and is to be used only to force a meeting. Keep notes and records of all communication, verbal or otherwise.

If all your attempts to settle the matter fail, proceed with the eviction notice. Eviction is a legal process, so if you haven't yet identified a great real estate attorney for your HOLD team, this is certainly the time. If you have an attorney, bring them up to speed on the situation and supply them with copies of all necessary documents. These documents may vary based on the circumstances but may include the lease, any correspondence with the tenant (notices, etc.), the tenant ledger, and forcible detainer. You may also want to include instructions to the attorney to file the judgment immediately, which will cause the issue of concern to be recorded on the tenant's credit report.

The attorney will obtain a court date and notify both parties of said date. The eviction notice instructs the tenants to discuss the matter with your attorney, to answer questions, or to make payment arrangements.

During the court hearing, the judge will assign the judgment, or the total dollar amount owed by the tenant for past due rent, fees, court costs, or damages, as well as a final vacating date. It takes about twenty days to evict a tenant in most states. Figure 13-12 shows all possible outcomes of going through the eviction process.

If	Then
The tenant pays the total amount of the judgment	The tenant may be allowed to stay, if you choose. If you don't want them to stay or the tenant elects to move out by the specified date, follow the tenant move-out procedure.
The tenant elects to make payments on the judgment amount, as determined by the court	The tenant must vacate the property by the date specified by the judge using the tenant move-out procedure.
The tenant does not pay the judgment, but moves out of the property	Instruct your attorney to record the judgment and turn the account over to a collection agency. The tenant forfeits all deposits.
The tenant refuses to move out of the property by the specified date	Instruct your attorney to file a writ with the court. Once the writ is filed, the constable's office is notified and they will contact you with a scheduled date to evict. You or someone from your office will have to meet the constable at the property on the scheduled date to forcibly evict the tenants.

Figure 13-12

None of these situations are pleasant, and we hope you never have to experience them firsthand. But it is important to know what could happen, how you can prevent it, and your options for a sound solution if you were to get caught up in a less-than-desirable situation. When you're a new investor or only own a few properties, this can seem manageable, but how do you know when to hand these matters over to someone else? That's where working with a property management company comes into play. We'll help you walk through this decision in the next segment.

Hire a Property Management Company ... or Not?

Jennice and Steve have run a successful property management business since 1979, and Jennice has been a professional property manager in both commercial and residential real estate for thirty-plus years. Still, neither one chooses to manage their own investment properties. Why? Because they know firsthand the challenges of managing rental property and they feel they have more productive uses for their time.

On the other hand, Jim and Linda managed their first 10 properties themselves before eventually hiring a property manager. "You have to have the tools and the team if you want to do it yourself," Jim says. "The idea of self-managing property is actually a myth." For Jim, this means having a system for conducting background and credit checks, a good lease that you understand fully, and a great handyman—nothing is too small to subcontract when you're a busy investor. You will also need a good real estate agent who can list your property for you in MLS and spend the time showing it to potential investors. Even if the agent charges half of the first month's rent, it's worth it not to have the property sit vacant, he says. Using a property management company can be expensive, but if you don't have the systems in place to do the job yourself, the advantages can far outweigh the expense.

The truth is some investors just aren't cut out to be property managers. One investor we know actually calls himself the worst property manager in existence. "I'm too soft-hearted," he says. "It wasn't until I hired a property manager that I started making money. Before, I was too cheap to pay the 10 percent, but 10 percent is cheap if it's increasing your income by 20 percent."

So how do you know when you and your team of experts can handle it and when to abandon ship? Consider the following factors to determine if hiring a property management company would be a good decision for your business. You should consider hiring a property management company if:

- **You live in a different town**

  If your rental property is located far from where you live, hiring a property management company can be invaluable in dealing with the many issues that you will not be able to handle from afar.

- **Your time is limited**

  Many investors view rental property ownership strictly as an investment and want little or nothing to do with the day-to-day management of their properties. Even if you do enjoy the process of finding good tenants, dealing with vendors, and maintaining a safe and attractive property, you may prefer to spend your time searching for new properties and growing your business.

- **You can afford the cost**

  Hiring a property management company is an attractive option if you can afford the fees—typically between 5 and 10 percent of what you collect in rent revenue. For many property owners, this is a small price to pay for the extra security of having a property management firm to act as your representative.

- **You have too many properties to manage alone**

  If your business is growing, at some point you may find that you need a substantial amount of help to manage everything properly. At that point, it might make sense to hire a property management company. Or you might grow your business to the point where you can do what Jim and Linda did and hire a property manager as part of your administration team.

Just remember, every investor is different. For some people, it's one event that leads them to seek outside help, like a first eviction or a water heater exploding. But if you're like most investors, it will be a series of events that will tell you when it's time to call on a property management firm.

POINTS TO REMEMBER

- When it comes to getting the most bang for your buck in real estate HOLDing, it's important to manage three key areas:

    - 1. finances

    - 2. maintenance and repairs

    - 3. tenants

- Every investor is different and has varying investment needs.

- All investors need to treat their investments as a small business and follow a set of guidelines.

In the following chapter, we'll delve deeper into your established financial structure to help you make sure to keep accurate records and run it like a business.

CHAPTER 14: RUN IT LIKE A BUSINESS

✓
3. BUY
An investment property where you make money going in

Outcome: a profitable property to add to your HOLD investment portfolio

↓

4. MANAGE
Your tenants and properties like a pro

☑ **Chapter 12**: Find Good Tenants

☑ **Chapter 13**: Increase Value

☐ **Chapter 14**: Run It Like a Business

Outcome: a sustainable investment property for your HOLD portfolio

After reading this chapter, you will know how to:

☐ Manage your records.

☐ Maximize your tax deductions.

☐ Minimize your risk and liability.

Your approach to being a property manager matters. If you treat it as a hobby, it will likely pay you as a hobby. However, if you run it like a business, you'll likely be far happier with your financial results. But what does that mean? The best businesses work from proven models and are systematic in their approach. It's a mindset, really. When you manage property like a business, you take things seriously enough to manage the details, not just the dreams. The details, in fact, often become the firm foundation upon which dreams are realized. Your visions of building wealth, adding to your annual cash flow, and someday achieving financial freedom are officially underway. But to realize these goals, you'll need to do some of the less glamorous work that all good businesses do. You'll need to keep detailed records, track expenses and capital investments for tax purposes, and manage against risk and liability.

In this chapter, we'll discuss some of the tools and systems that are available to help you manage your rental properties like a business. We'll show you how to organize your records and we'll explain some of the tax deductions available to owners of rental properties. Finally, we'll explain how you can reduce the risks and liabilities that come with property management.

MANAGE YOUR RECORDS

One area where many investors fall short is recordkeeping. Keeping accurate records for a rental property is essential for any landlord. Records help you avoid discrimination claims, prevent misunderstandings about the property's condition, and manage your expenses and deductions.

Those of us who have been in this business for a while probably started our property management with the help of a Dome Rental Property Record book. Available at just about any office supply store, this book was a remarkably efficient way to maintain a detailed handwritten account of monthly income, expenses, rents, and fees for one to four projects and up to sixty units.

While Dome worked well for us during our beginnings—and we know investors who swear by it to this day—there are now many more sophisticated options available. For less than $200, software such as Quicken's Rental Property Manager helps you organize and manage your personal and rental property finances, track income, expenses, and tax deductions. It allows you to see which tenants have paid and which ones owe you money, all while keeping detailed records of your properties. These records include contents, vacancies, advertising history, mortgage and insurance, and repairs. At the end of the year, you can quickly generate year-to-date income and expenses and a detailed general ledger to submit to your accountant when it is time to file your taxes.

We're not trying to sell you a software package. That's just one we know well. In truth, as technologies move to the cloud and software apps abound, there are numerous affordable options available to you. We simply recommend that you include your CPA or bookkeeper in the final selection process. One CPA shared with us, "I have three rates for filing returns. There's the rate for a bunch of receipts and pay stubs in a shoe box, there's the rate for a homemade spreadsheet, and then the rate for a real P&L and ledger." It's something to think about. If your record keeping solution is forcing your CPA to spend two to three extra hours just it into something they can work with, you may spend more

cost of any software when it comes time to file your tax return.

rdless of your method of choice, it's important to know what you

eed to track when it comes to your investment properties.

Know What to Record

There are literally hundreds of things to track on your properties. Depending on how you look at things, it can be an overwhelming experience or actually quite simple. We prefer the later. Almost everything you can imagine actually falls into four big buckets: income, expenses, tenants, and properties. So while you can break these down as far as you like, you could also keep it simple in the beginning and then add levels of organization as you grow more comfortable in your role.

1. Track your income

Keeping a documented record of your income is very important. Again, think of your investments as a separate business and your income as your paycheck. The government will be looking to tax certain dollar amounts, and it's important to keep your own record for comparison. Remember, this includes all rental income including fees.

2. Track your expenses separately for each property

Your number one expense will almost certainly be your monthly mortgage principal and interest payments, property taxes and insurance. These are often referred to as your PITI (principal, interest, taxes, and insurance) and are often bundled into one payment by your mortgage lender. Expenses can include maintenance work, equipment, or furniture purchased for the property, such as new fixtures, plus all repair and cleaning costs. If you hire a property management company, keep records of your payments. If certain expenses apply to all your properties—such as legal, accounting, mileage, or travel—you can split those costs evenly.

3. Track your tenants

For each of your tenants, keep a separate file containing a copy of their signed lease agreement, an initialed copy of the walk-through checklist, and a record of rental payments. You will also want to record and track any problems or claims from your tenants, along with warnings or notices that you have given them. In the event you ever have to evict someone, this file should include all the documentation needed when serving the eviction notice.

4. Track your properties

When you closed on 742 Evergreen Terrace, the closing officer or attorney provided you with copies of all your closing documents. At the very least, you're property files should include these important documents. If you or the seller purchases a home warranty, that goes in the file too. Hopefully, you kept a copy of your inspection report. If not, contact your real estate agent and ask them to help you obtain a copy. This a great starting point for your maintenance and repair records. The inspector will have noted the age or condition of all the house's major systems (e.g., the roof, the HVAC, etc.) and from this you can begin a planning form for future or planned repairs. We keep a punch list of needed improvements in our files so that when we have a vacancy we can get everything lined up for a quick turnaround.

MAXIMIZE YOUR DEDUCTIONS

As mentioned earlier, another reason to keep records is for deductions. Among the greatest benefits of owning rental real estate are the numerous tax advantages you receive. More deductions and tax-related strategies are available for this property than for just about any other type of investment.

There are the more obvious advantages like mortgage interest, but did you know that you can also write off all other operating expenses—like utilities, insurance, homeowner association fees, repairs and maintenance, and yard care—as well as the costs associated with conducting a real estate business at home?

The key, however, is to keep detailed records of all rental-related activities, including receipts and invoices. Property management software programs can help you organize these records to simplify tax preparation. And you will want to consult with your accountant for specific guidelines, but here are some of the biggest tax advantages we've found.

Please note that all tax benefits should be seen as icing and not the cake. In the past, when investors have let tax considerations drive their purchase decisions, it has generally ended poorly. Why? Tax law changes. If you want proof, look no further than The Tax Reform Act of 1986 in the United States, which retroactively removed some huge tax benefits from investment real estate and created ruin for investors who purchased property for that reason alone. So, while you should absolutely capitalize on the tax advantages of owning investment properties, never allow them to overshadow the sound HOLD analysis principle we shared earlier. It's cash flow first, appreciation second, and tax benefits last.

Here are seven of the top deductions we focus on each year. Please review them with your CPA to see which of them you can take advantage of. In Canada, investors enjoy many rebates and deductions, especially at the point of sale, but their tax code is quite different. Canadians should absolutely consult with their HOLD team about the special tax considerations they can enjoy.

1. Depreciation

One of the best tax tools for a landlord, depreciation allows you to write off your biggest expense: the purchase price for the rental property. What's more, you can depreciate the cost of residential buildings over 27.5 years, even while they are increasing in value. You get to depreciate the property because of wear and tear, deterioration, or obsolescence of the property. You don't however, get to depreciate the land under your house—dirt doesn't wear out, after all. As an example, let's revisit your property on 742 Evergreen Terrace. You bought it for $135,000, of which, $25,000 was the appraised value of the land. So in year one, if nothing else entered the equation, the basis for your appreciation deduction would be $110,000 ($135,000 sale price less $25,000 for the land.). Divide by 27.5 and you get an annual appreciation deduction of $4,000.

In addition, you can also depreciate the various components of a property and its improvements. Furniture and appliances, for instance, are depreciated over five years. Property improvements are also depreciated over time, although the cost of most repairs is deductible only in the year when it is incurred.

The difference between an improvement and a repair is that improvements add to the value of a property by prolonging its useful life or adapting it to new uses. When you repair something, you are simply making sure your property remains in good condition. The cost of repairs to rental property is fully deductible in the year in which the costs are incurred. Examples of deductible repairs include repainting, fixing gutters or floors, repairing leaks, plastering, and replacing broken windows.

2. Operating Expenses

Routine expenses that keep a property operational shouldn't be overlooked. For instance, you can claim deductions for financing a rental property including mortgage interest payments and private mortgage insurance. You can also deduct interest on loans for improvements. Other allowable deductions include local property taxes, property management fees, advertising, and utilities if the tenants aren't paying for them. Property association dues, landscaping, and garbage pickup are also eligible. Just remember to keep accurate records of each.

If you hire anyone to perform services for your rental property, you can deduct their wages as a rental business expense. This is true whether the worker is an employee or an independent contractor.

3. Insurance

You can deduct the premiums paid for almost any policy, including fire, theft, and flood insurance for rental property, as well as landlord liability insurance. If you have employees, you can deduct the cost of their health and workers' compensation insurance as well.

4. Home Office

Provided they meet certain requirements, you may deduct your home office expenses as an investor from your taxable income. This deduction applies not only to space devoted to office work, but also to any other home workspace you use for your rental business. This is true whether you own your home or apartment or are a renter, but keep in mind that the space must be used exclusively for your business and for no other purpose. This would exclude the dining room table.

That being said, even if you don't meet the home-office criteria, you can still deduct ordinary business expenses you incur at home like long-distance phone calls and office supplies.

5. Services

Fees that you pay to attorneys, accountants, property management companies, real estate investment advisers, and other professionals can all be counted as service fees. You can deduct these as operating expenses as long as the fees are paid for work related to your rental activity.

6. Travel

You can deduct travel expenses associated with your rental property, whether it involves driving across town or flying across the country. For local travel, deduct gasoline, upkeep, repairs, and mileage, using the standard mileage rate. Tolls and parking are also deductible. If you travel overnight for your rental activity, you can deduct your airfare, hotel bills, meals, and other expenses. IRS auditors closely scrutinize deductions for overnight travel. To stay within the law, you need to properly document your long distance travel expenses.

7. Losses

If your rental property is damaged or destroyed from a sudden event like a fire or flood, you may be able to obtain a tax deduction for all or part of your loss. How much you may deduct depends on the extent of the damage and whether the loss was covered by insurance. It is important to track all damages and losses carefully so that you can arrive at a deduction possibility after speaking with your insurance agent.

RISK MANAGEMENT

Aside from helping you achieve tax breaks, keeping accurate records will also help you avoid risk. Just like any business, as a rental property manager you need to manage your risk. An accident, disaster, or lawsuit can threaten the economic viability of your property.

There are a number of ways you can organize and control your business to minimize the adverse effects of accidental loss, starting with how you structure your business. The possibilities would include a sole proprietorship, a limited liability company (LLC), or a corporation. Because laws vary from state to state and between the U.S. and Canada, we recommend that you seek professional advice.

And when it comes to lease agreements, you should make sure they specify all indemnities, liabilities, and any other stipulations that could present hazards. You can list these as separate items that require signatures or initials from the tenants, verifying that they have seen the stipulations and agree to them.

Meticulous documentation of all activities and tenant interaction is also a must. You can counter any legal action if there are detailed records that disprove their claims.

You will also want to obtain insurance coverage for potential hazards. Landlords insurance is designed to protect a property from financial losses resulting from disasters ranging from fires, earthquakes, storms, or floods to explosions, theft, and malicious damage. Insurance costs are higher for rental property—about 15 to 20 percent more than regular homeowner policies because the owner doesn't have exclusive control over the property. As we've already discussed, you will need to consult your insurance agent to decide which coverage is best for you as each insurance policy is different. But you generally have at least these three options to choose from: 1. lost rental income, 2. liability, and 3. property contents.

1. Lost Rental Income

If your rental property is damaged, the costs of repair are not the only factor you have to consider. Repairs take time, and in many cases the property cannot be occupied while it is being restored. Depending on the terms of the policy you select, loss of rent coverage will pay you a certain amount of money up to a maximum period of time while the property is being repaired. If you're dependent on rental income to cover your mortgage payments, this type of coverage can be a lifesaver.

2. Liability

You may also want to consider additional forms of coverage, such as liability coverage and/or an umbrella policy. These policies can protect you when things go really wrong, such as a tenant or one of their guests being seriously injured at your property. If tenants can prove that the injury was due to the landlord's negligence they can file a personal injury lawsuit or claim against the landlord's insurance company for medical bills, lost earnings, pain and suffering, permanent physical disability and disfigurement, and emotional distress. A tenant can also sue for damage to personal property if they can provide that it is the result of faulty maintenance or unsafe conditions. This heightened liability coverage and umbrella policy provides a layer of protection for your personal assets should anything happen and a lawsuit be filed.

3. Property Contents

Landlords insurance policies typically cover your own belongings that tenants might use, such as appliances, carpets, equipment, and furnishings. Be sure to take an accurate inventory of your personal effects on the premises, and purchase enough landlord insurance to cover all of your belongings.

While landlords insurance is not a legal requirement, it will provide you with the peace of mind that comes from knowing that, should disaster strike, you are protected against financial consequences. Without it, you run the risk of losing your valuable investment and owing hundreds of thousands of dollars in repairs or legal fees and judgments. And, to take things a step further, we'll remind you to include renters insurance for your tenants in the terms of your lease agreement.

At the end of the day, running your investment property like a business is less overwhelming than many might think. In the weeks after purchase there are indeed a lot of things to get organized, but that is also when you are most excited about your big investment. Believe us when we tell you that knowing you've made a great financial investment takes the sting out of most of the chores. The truth is, for those who take the time to manage their properties like a business, their commitment is rewarded by significantly higher wages.

Having tackled the basics of property management for your own 742 Evergreen Terrace investment, it's time to contemplate the future. In the next part, Grow, we'll talk about the journey from your first investment property to developing a portfolio of cash flow properties.

POINTS TO REMEMBER

- Accurate recordkeeping of tenants, income, and expenses is essential for successful property management. It achieves the following:

  - Simplifies tax returns and maximizes deductions.

  - Protects you from discrimination claims and prevents misunderstandings about the property's condition.

  - Helps you manage expenses and profit goals.

- Rental property ownership has more tax benefits and strategies than any other business.

  - Depreciate the cost of residential buildings more than 27.5 years, even while they are increasing in value.

  - Depreciate improvements (things that add value to a property by prolonging its useful life or adapting it to new uses).

  - Deduct cost of repairs (in the year the repair was made).

  - Deduct the cost of doing business (home office, travel, salaries, and professional services).

- Risk management strategies can make or break a property rental business. These include:

  - How you structure your business (corporation, partnership, LLC).

  - How you write your lease to cover contingencies.

  - How you insure against loss and liability.

✓	**1. FIND**
	The right property for the right terms and the right price

Outcome: a list of qualified investment properties from which to choose

↓

✓	**2. ANALYZE**
	A property to make sure the numbers and the terms make sense

Outcome: a prospect that meets your financial criteria

↓

✓	**3. BUY**
	An investment property where you make money going in

Outcome: a profitable property to add to your HOLD investment portfolio

↓

✓	**4. MANAGE**
	Your tenants and properties like a pro

Outcome: a sustainable investment property for your HOLD portfolio

↓

5. GROW
Your way to wealth and financial freedom

☐ **Chapter 15**: Manage to the Goal

☐ **Chapter 16**: Models for Growth

Outcome: an investment portfolio that funds the life you want to live

To accomplish great things, we must not only act, but also dream;
not only plan, but also believe.

ANATOLE FRANCE

We've now come to the part of the journey where you begin to fully realize the wealth-creation potential of the HOLD model. And that means it's time to expand. The Grow phase of your journey actually begins when you buy and take possession of your very first rental property—and it can extend throughout your lifetime. It doesn't happen by chance, and it doesn't happen in a far-off distant future. It starts now.

In fact, as you've made your way through each phase of the HOLD process, you've been growing. You are enhancing your knowledge, expanding your network, and growing in discipline and discernment. This is when things can really get interesting..

Some investors will buy one, two, or even three properties and go no further. A manageable number of investment properties will satisfy the modest goals these investors have set for themselves. Maybe you're one of them. But for other investors—like us and maybe you too—Grow means going even bigger. You see, as we acquired more properties, our wealth grew and we grew with it. And we discovered new opportunities that either we hadn't seen before or weren't available to us at that stage in the journey. As we explored these new avenues to financial wealth, we acquired new skills and new knowledge, which in turn opened the doors to other opportunities.

The thing about this phase of the HOLD strategy is that it's as dynamic as it is circular—you're always at some stage of the process, although it gets easier as you go along. It's like beginning a workout program. It may be hard at first, but as you get stronger and fitter, you find that you can do it faster, more efficiently, and even achieve more in a lot less time. The Grow stage of investing works a lot like any other goal in life. Once you set your goal, the results come faster and faster as long as you remain committed.

It all begins when you take time to evaluate the goals you started with. You'll need to know if you're on the right track. You might need to make some adjustments or try some new strategies. In these chapters we're going to share how to manage to the goals you set. We'll share insights and successful Grow strategies to open your mind to new investment possibilities. And we'll give you some proven techniques for managing your portfolio over time.

Remember, the Grow phase is when the fun and rewards of investing in a HOLD strategy really kick in. Get ready to enjoy your successes and walk a new path to achieve more!

CHAPTER 15: MANAGE TO THE GOAL

✓	**4. MANAGE** **Your tenants and properties like a pro**

Outcome: a sustainable investment property for your HOLD portfolio

5. GROW
Your way to wealth and financial freedom

☐ **Chapter 15**: Manage to the Goal

☐ **Chapter 16**. Models for Growth

Outcome: an investment portfolio that funds the life you want to live

After reading this chapter, you will know how to:

☐ Define long-term goals for your financial wealth.

☐ Perform routine goal checkups.

☐ Leverage your network to overcome obstacles along the way.

Think back to the goals you set when you explored your financial criteria in "Find." Were you most focused on growing your cash flow or your net worth? Why was it important? Was it freedom from the stress of living paycheck to paycheck, increased confidence in your retirement savings, or maybe creating a college fund for your kids? On our wealth-building journey, we've found that our initial goals (that seemed barely achievable in the beginning) mostly turned out to be too small. And along the way, we had to adopt a bigger vision of what was possible for our lives. We want to encourage you to look beyond your initial goals and think bigger now.

In *The Millionaire Real Estate Investor*, Gary Keller defined financial wealth as the "unearned income to finance your life mission without having to work." It's what most would call financial freedom. What would your life look like if you had all the money you needed and could spend your days doing whatever you like? That's the ultimate growth path, because no matter how big or small your financial vision might be, it's just right for you. Regardless of what your financial vision might be, it doesn't happen by accident. There's a process to follow if you want to take luck out of the equation.

When you picked up this book and began your journey, you likely had a vision. Now it's time to use a proven process to take stock of where you are, where you want to be, and how to get there.

THE FINANCIAL GAP ANALYSIS

Over the years, we've helped hundreds, if not thousands, of people set bigger and better financial goals for their life. It's simply a consultative process. We ask three fundamental questions and work together to discover the best possible answers.

1. Define Your Goal – What does financial wealth look like for you, and when will you achieve it?

2. Take Stock of Your Starting Point – Where are you today?

3. Bridge the Gap – Working backward, how do we go from here to there?

1. Define Your Goal

To achieve your goal, you have to first define your goal. While it sounds pretty obvious, you'd be surprised by how few people actually take the time to do this. One great piece of advice the McKissacks always offer people is, "If you don't know what your perfect life looks like or how much it costs, you won't be able to set goals to achieve it." There are two parts to this philosophy: You have to envision your perfect life, then calculate the costs. Most people stop with the vision.

We like to think of the goal-setting process as practical dreaming—the emphasis on practical. For most, the perfect life isn't really about owning your own island and having a fleet of Bentleys at your beck and call. It's about having a house paid for, maybe owning a second home somewhere you cherish, and having the excess money to travel, shop, buy gifts for, and spend time with the people you love. That's a life you can probably visualize in surprising detail and do a pretty decent job of estimating the amount of wealth it would require.

When Jim and Linda bought their first real estate property, Jim was almost forty years old. The two of them knew that one day they wanted to have the freedom to walk away from working. Their goal was to have enough real estate investments to earn $20,000 a month in passive income by the time Jim reached retirement age around 65. If you do the math, that's $240,000 a year in passive investment income, and they had roughly twenty-five years to achieve it.

For your financial wealth goals to become a reality, you need to reach this level of clarity as well. This is a crystal ball exercise. No one knows how much anything will cost in the future, so don't get too hung up on nailing down the cost of things to the penny. Just take whatever number you dream up, maybe its $100,000 in annual passive income to finance your big financial wealth goal and start by doubling it. That's right. Double it.

The idea is that if you can build a plan in step 3 of this process to accomplish twice your original goal, it will erase almost any mistakes you may have made. As a bonus, by thinking big, even if you fall a little short, you may find yourself achieving things well beyond your original vision. Thinking big does that.

2. Take Stock of Your Starting Point

The second step is the easiest—you need to define your starting point. If you want to get to Pittsburgh, the journey is defined by the point of departure. If you live in Cleveland, no sweat. If you're based in Shanghai, you're going to take a far different kind of journey.

Earlier in this book, we discussed net worth. We believe it's the greatest measure of financial success. In *The Millionaire Real Estate Investor*, Gary says tracking your net worth on a monthly basis should become a fundamental habit of your new investor lifestyle. We agree. It's the kind of habit that always lets you know exactly where you stand financially, and it also encourages you to acquire assets while avoiding unnecessary debt.

As you probably remember, your net worth is the sum total of everything you own minus everything you owe. When you applied for your mortgage to purchase 742 Evergreen Terrace, the mortgage application was, in effect, a net worth worksheet. It's time to repeat that exercise. Revisit your financial records and add up all your assets, including your new investment property. Then tally up all your debt, which now includes the mortgage on your rental property. When you subtract your debt from your assets, you'll know your starting point.

Classic wisdom from retirement experts is that you need to take the income it would take to live your preferred lifestyle and save twenty times that before retirement. For example, the McKissacks set a goal of $240,000 in annual passive income. If they started from a net worth of zero, one route to achieve that would be to accumulate investments that buoyed their net worth to $4.8 million (20 x $240,000). Once they found their big number, they would calculate the amount and kinds of assets to buy today that would grow in value to hit their target on time. That, of course, assumes no cash flow. Over time, they would have to sell their assets to finance their lifestyle and hope they got it right.

While there is nothing inherently wrong with this very common approach, we define financial wealth in terms of "unearned income."

To calculate your starting point for unearned income, simply add up all your passive income. For most people, this doesn't take long. Maybe they have an interest-bearing savings account or own stocks that pay regular dividends, but that's it. There isn't much to add up. But don't be discouraged. Knowing your starting point is essential to building your wealth.

The good news is that with your successful acquisition of 742 Evergreen Terrace, you do have some meaningful cash flow. If you revisit the HOLD Property Analysis Worksheet, you see that you now enjoy over $800 a year in passive income. In fifteen years, with regular rent appreciation, you may have more than $6,000 in annual cash flow. And by the time the property matures and the debt has been completely paid down, you'll be looking at as much as $15,000 in annual net cash flow. Congrats, you're off to a good start!

On the other hand, when the McKissacks started buying houses in the early '90s, they were like everybody else: working hard and not saving much. They had a tall hill to climb but they also had twenty-five years to make the journey.

3. Bridge the Gap

This is the fun part. Once you know where you want to be someday and where you are today, you can devise a plan to get you there. It's the process of working backward from a big goal until you are staring at something manageable.

For the McKissacks, despite having a twenty-five year plan, they broke their goals down to the point where all they had to focus on was saving a $20,000 down payment as fast as they could. It's not a small goal but it was simple and actionable, which probably contributed to their eventual success.

To achieve their goal of $20,000 in monthly passive income, the McKissacks centered on purchasing investment properties in their hometown of Denton, Texas. They focused on properties in attractive, stable neighborhoods for at least 10 percent below the market value that created a cash flow of at least $200 a month from day one. At that time, the McKissacks could buy a 3-bedroom brick house for $115,000 that was worth $130,000—a little more than 10 percent below market value—put 20 percent down, and finance it for $92,000 on a 15-year note. Renting it for $1,200 a month, they could cash flow a couple hundred dollars a month over and above the mortgage payment, taxes, and insurance.

By purchasing properties on 15-year notes and using all the cash flow to accelerate the debt pay down, they felt they could achieve their big financial goal by owning 20 properties that each had a monthly cash flow of $1,000 after all expenses. At the end of the journey, they'd have $20,000 a month in unearned income.

With a clear vision for their goal, they broke it down into logical steps. They needed a path to their goal. So they set out to buy two properties the first year and finance them for 15 years; four properties the second year; and ramping up to five or six acquisitions in the fifth year. That way, by the end of those first five years, they would acquire 20 properties, pay them off within twenty years of their start date, and have their goal income secured by the time Jim reached sixty. Notice that their plan was bigger than the minimum required. They could have created a plan that took twenty-five years but chose instead to design one that took twenty. They thought big.

That's all well and good, but saying you're going to buy two properties a year is one thing—affording them is another. The McKissacks kept working through their goal and even decided to set up an automatic savings plan. Fifteen percent of every commission check from Linda's real estate business and the cash flow from all the properties they owned would go directly into a money market account. They would learn how to live off 85 percent of their income. Whenever their money market account reached $20,000, they'd use it as a down payment on another property.

Doing it the slow, steady-Eddie way—putting money away until they had enough to put a sizable down payment on the property—it wasn't long before they had built up so much equity, learned so much, and their income had grown so much that $20,000 a month no longer seemed like the magic number. They blew through their goals—at one point, they owned more than 100 properties.

Not only that, as they learned more about real estate investing, new opportunities came their way. They were having so much fun building and managing their business that retiring at sixty didn't seem so desirable. So they broadened their goal, bought several real estate companies and pursued new business opportunities.

Now it's your turn. Take your big financial vision and see if you can plot a path from where you are today to the someday you most want to live. You can use the free HOLD Property Analysis Worksheet (www.KellerINK.com) to mock up a bread-and-butter investment property in your market area. How many would you have to acquire to reach your goals? Please note that on the second tab of the worksheet, we'll take your assumptions about appreciation, cash flow, and rents out thirty years for you. That's not easy math. We understand. And while no one knows the future, these numbers can still serve as the basis for your Financial Gap Analysis.

This is a great time to enlist your HOLD team of advisers. Invite them to poke holes in your plan. Ask how they would go about it. Most should be happy to help. You've got your real estate agent, your property manager, your CPA, and your attorney, and all the other people on your team who can lend you their experience and expertise in the pursuit of your goals. We know one investor that assembled her advisers each year for dinner for the sole purpose of sharing her goals. This may in fact be when you discover your first investment mentor—that person who truly takes you under their wing and takes a vested interest in your success. It happens more often than you might think. We know because mentoring investors is a passion we share and one of the more rewarding things we do.

PERFORM ROUTINE GOAL CHECKUPS

Your job as the investor is to ask questions. Ask yourself, "What is my goal, what am I wanting to achieve from my investment strategy, and am I still on the right path for achieving it?" You will need to ask your team questions too. Talk to your property manager and ask if you are getting the rent expected. Ask about developments in the neighborhood—are the property values still trending the way you thought they would, or have things changed? Maybe the property manager has a client that doesn't want to hold onto their house anymore, giving you an opportunity to purchase another property that already has a tenant in it. Talk to your real estate agent and find out what's happening in your target areas. Find out from your CPA if there are any new tax considerations or investing strategies. Asking the right questions will ensure you stay focused on your goal. This type of evaluation should become a regular annual or semi-annual exercise.

As you perform your evaluation, you'll likely think the investment part was way easier than you might have initially imagined. If all proceeds smoothly on your property, you might be ready to say, "Let's do it again." All the analysis, spadework, and sacrifices you made up front have borne fruit. Now the fun part starts, and the opportunities are even bigger. In order to make a lasting success or achievement, you become something different in the process.

It may sound funny, but the hardest thing for some investors is to stick to their own goals and not get caught up in someone else's. You may know someone who does a lot of flips because they live in an area where there's a lot of appreciation. Don't get caught up in someone else's goals because they sound good. Stay clear about what you want.

Smart investors create systems and strategies they can successfully duplicate over and over again. In other words, once you find a winning system, nine times out of ten you should stick with it. There is a real benefit to repetition—it's built expertise. The more duplexes you purchase in your market, the more mastery you'll achieve on investing in duplexes. It's a big advantage. We know investors who can walk into a property and, without looking at the listing information, tell you who the builder was, when it was built, the general layout, and the five things to look out for in those kinds of properties. Because of their accumulated knowledge, they can make great investment decisions at light speed.

At the same time, it's okay if your goals change. In most cases, investors evolve. They are changing out of heightened goals or sheer boredom. As they grow as investors and their wealth accumulates, new opportunities become available that weren't options in the past. You have to give yourself the freedom to evolve when, after careful evaluation, a different track makes sense.

LEVERAGE YOUR NETWORK TO OVERCOME OBSTACLES

Part of managing to the goal is to understand what obstacles will arise. Getting started is the hardest part, but you will hit the barriers to progress along the way. Make your plan and work your plan. Just remember that surprises occur, so be prepared with a plan B, a plan C, or even a plan D. This is when your network can be your most valuable asset.

For example, when Jim started purchasing properties at foreclosure sales, he discovered a circle of supportive and knowledgeable investors at the auctions who were willing to exchange information about different properties and offer advice.

If you're surrounding yourself with other people who are buying and investing in property, you'll feel more comfortable about investing. Build your HOLD network. Join investor clubs, take classes, read books—the support you need to keep moving toward your goals is all around you once you make the commitment and strike out to find it.

Here's what we know: Everybody dreams about having more—few plan to make it happen. The best investors always do—and they do it by defining their vision, reevaluating their goals, and enlisting a powerful network to help them along the way.

POINTS TO REMEMBER

- You started with a vision of what you wanted to achieve. Define it in as much detail as you can imagine. What does it look like? When will you achieve it? How much will that life cost to fund?

- Perform regular goal checkups. Goals can change depending on your lifestyle and circumstance. Revisit your goals periodically and see if they still work for you.

- Stay focused. Smart investors create models and stick with them. Repetition can be beautiful and profitable.

- Prepare for change. No matter how much you work to achieve your goal, life sometimes intervenes. If you have developed discipline and a commitment to learning you can weather the change and discover new opportunities.

- Build your network of HOLD professionals with a purpose. Although you can't list them on your net worth sheet, there are few things that will make your net worth grow more or faster than a powerful network of allies.

CHAPTER 16: MODELS FOR GROWTH

✓ | **4. MANAGE**
Your tenants and properties like a pro

Outcome: a sustainable investment property for your HOLD portfolio

5. GROW
Your way to wealth and financial freedom

☑ **Chapter 15**: Manage to the Goal

☐ **Chapter 16**: Models for Growth

Outcome: an investment portfolio that funds the life you want to live

After reading this chapter, you will know how to:

☐ Look for and finance new investment opportunities.

☐ Leverage existing investments to expand your portfolio.

GROW YOUR PORTFOLIO

One of the most powerful things about expanding your real estate investment portfolio is that once you commit to it and pursue it with diligence and faith, more and better opportunities appear. The more wealth you accumulate, the more opportunities you have to pursue. The more people who know you are a real estate investor, the more opportunities they will send your way. There is a virtuous cycle that can come into play. And sometimes, even a marginal investment managed well can evolve into a monumental asset over time.

Steve Chader bought a two-bedroom investment property when his son was four to pay for his future college education. Even though the property at the time of purchase guaranteed a small amount of negative cash flow, Steve did the math and realized he'd have to invest more in a traditional college fund to even have a chance at covering the cost of university education. He was also confident he would be able to raise rents over time and raise the overall performance of the property. He was right. As time went on, the property cash flowed $300 a month, and Steve used the money to advance the property debt pay down. By the time his son was eighteen, Steve had reached his goal and that lone property could pay for all four years of college.

But Steve's son ended up not wanting to go to a four-year school. So Steve looked at his long-term investment and changed his goal. He sold the property using a 1031 exchange to defer his tax liability from the sale and bought two new properties: a triplex and a three-bedroom, single-family home. This increased his monthly cash flow further, and he used the extra income to pay down both mortgages even faster than before. Then he sold those properties using a 1031 exchange and bought an office building. Though a commercial office building was never in his original plan, as his investment portfolio grew, so did Steve's vision. In fact, he continues to grow his portfolio and wealth even today.

Similarly, Jennice once took over a rental from an investor whose property she managed. The property had taken on a negative cash flow and the investor could no longer afford it. She offered it to Jennice, who took over the monthly payments and acquired the property with no money down. Jennice still owns the now cash flowing property today.

So how do you continue to fund opportunities that spring up unexpectedly? How do you leverage what you already own to build your portfolio? And what are the strategies you can use to increase the value of your holdings?

In this chapter, we'll discuss some of the ways you can grow your investments through funding new opportunities or leveraging your current properties. Just remember, investment models are very much area specific. What works for the McKissacks in their target market in north Texas may not work for an investor in a market in southern California or central Colorado. Furthermore, the strategy you use today may need to change, depending on the market cycle. Regardless, the money and means to achieve your dreams are out there. All you have to do is find them.

FUND NEW OPPORTUNITIES

If there's one thing you should have learned by now: When it comes to growing your investments there's more than one way to skin a cat. Real estate investors are crafty. They think outside the box and are always looking for new opportunities. You too will begin sniffing out new prospects more and more as you continue to grow your portfolio. Over the years, we've come across many, many transactions—some riskier than others—but these three strategies remain tried-and-true ways to fund your growth: 1. leave an investment trail, 2. buy real estate with an IRA, and 3. turn necessary expenses into gains.

1. Leave an Investment Trail

A great way to build your real estate portfolio is through the owner-occupied model. As we discussed earlier in "Buy," you can purchase a property as the primary resident with the intent to HOLD it as an investment when you're ready to trade up. This way, you can get the best mortgage interest rates possible, save money on remodeling by doing it yourself, probably have a smaller down payment, and pay down your mortgage for a few years while you save for your next down payment.

The important thing is to buy it like an investment and, as you live in it, treat it like one as well. Any improvements you make should be done with your future renters in mind. For example, as you update the kitchen, you might opt for durable laminate countertops over granite and select mid-grade appliances instead of stainless steel ones fit for a commercial kitchen. You'll save thousands while making your current home even more attractive to future renters. And the thousands you keep in your bank account will accelerate your journey to your next down payment.

If you're younger or just willing, you can start collecting rental income long before you move out: you can get a roommate(s). Sign them on to a formal lease and the income will work for you when you try to qualify for your next property. It's not uncommon to find investors renting rooms out and covering most or all of their monthly payment. If a roommate isn't for you, you can consider short-term rentals. Renting your house out for just a week while you're on vacation can go a long way toward making that month's mortgage payment. We've known investors who have rented storage space in their garages for antique car owners, leased space in their yard to boat owners, and just about anything else you can imagine. It's your house: It's up to you. Steve bought a duplex as his first property, lived in one side and rented the other. This way he was able to save more quickly to buy his next house.

Even if you make this your only portfolio-building strategy, you can continue to acquire properties every three to five years at the best available rates, and leave a trail of cash-flowing investments behind to leverage as you choose.

2. Buy Real Estate with an IRA

Using a little-known IRS provision, investors can use tax-deferred retirement funds to invest in real estate. Section 408 of the Internal Revenue Code permits individuals to purchase land, commercial property, condominiums, residential property, trust deeds, or real estate contracts through various types of IRAs, including a traditional IRA, a Roth IRA, a Simplified Employee Pension plan, or a 401(k). This allows you to take money out of the stock market and reinvest it in properties—often referred to as a "real estate IRA," or a "self-directed IRA."

But since buying a property may require more funds than you currently have available in your IRA, you can also have your IRA purchase an interest in a property in conjunction with other individuals, such as a spouse, business associate, or friend. Internal Revenue Service regulations will not let you use the real estate owned by your IRA as your residence, vacation home, or business lease space. But, you can withdraw real estate from your IRA and use it as a residence or second home when you reach retirement age—around 59 or older for a penalty-free withdrawal.

There are other stipulations and limitations, which is why it's important to consult with your HOLD team and find an independent IRA custodian that specializes in real estate. Do an Internet search for "real estate IRA" or "self-directed IRA," a term coined by the financial industry in the 1980s to distinguish the self-directed IRA from IRAs that focus on stocks and bonds.

So why do investors go to all the trouble to move money from one investment to the next? A higher rate of return is the answer. Part of being an investor is always asking how hard your money is working. If you can achieve higher rates of return with equal or less risk, your answer should always be to trade up. Most retirement vehicles are low yield. At best, you might expect to grow your money at 10 to 12 percent on an annual basis. More often, you would probably be happy with a 7 to 8 percent annual rate of return. But as you now know, direct investment in HOLD real estate can deliver much higher yields while still enjoying the same tax benefits of the original IRA.

3. Turn Necessary Expenses into Gains

Another great way to fund a new investment opportunity is to look at where housing expenses may already or one day exist in your life. For example, if you have children that are going away to college—or even in the same town for that matter—they'll need a place to live. Yes, dorms or apartments are an option, but what if you could take that $8,000 a year boarding cost and turn it into a gain? You can.

Buy a single family home in a college town, let your child live there as a property manager, and have a few of her friends sign leases to rent the other rooms in the house. While your daughter's friends are paying down the mortgage, she is learning the ins and outs of real estate investment, property management, and adult living, all while attaining a college degree. Just think how much of the mortgage will have been paid by renters by the time your daughter graduates.

And at graduation, you can reassess the property and decide how best to leverage it. One way would be to gift it to your daughter as her first real estate investment. Another would be to continue HOLDing it and use the cash flow to invest in other opportunities. You could also sell or exchange the property—hopefully at an appreciated price—and reinvest the money from the sale. Any way you slice it, you will have taken a necessary cost and turned it into a win by making an investment and profit off of the initial expense.

That brings us to leverage. As we said earlier in this section, your goals and opportunities will continue to change and expand as you grow your portfolio. As this happens, you'll stumble upon models for leveraging your current properties to reach your new goals.

LEVERAGE YOUR CURRENT PROPERTIES

Just as reliable as finding new funding for portfolio growth, there are many ways to use your current investments to acquire new properties. Again, there are a variety of methods for this, and some are much more detailed and take many more years of investment expertise, so we recommend you consult your HOLD team before proceeding with any decisions. Some leveraging strategies are more straightforward than others, and it's important to be aware of these possibilities so that as you revisit your net worth, goals, or notice that house on the corner hit the market, you're prepared to take action. A few of the models that continue to work for us and many investors are: 1. tap your equity, 2. repurpose your existing properties, and 3. trade up with a 1031 exchange.

1. Tap Your Equity

Over time, as you evaluate the performance of your investment properties, you'll notice a curious thing. As you increasingly pay down the debt on a property, your money isn't working as hard. Your return on investment may still be high, but your return on equity falls with every mortgage payment. When your return on equity hits a certain threshold, you may want to pull some of it out and get the power of financial leverage working for you again.

To illustrate the difference between return on investment and return on equity, let's say your original cash investment of $20,000 now returns you $10,000 a year in net cash flow. That's a wonderful 50 percent annual return on your investment. But you bought the property thiry years ago and now you've paid down all the debt. With the house now worth $200,000, all the money you have tied to that property isn't working as hard as your original investment. If you consider your $200,000 equity position as potential cash to invest, you realize that $10,000 a year is only a 5 percent rate of return. That's a fine return if you simply want to keep your wealth safe. If you're still focused on growth, you may want to consider alternatives.

Investors can pull money out of the property by selling it, but there are alternatives to discarding an otherwise great asset. You can refinance the property and pull out some of your equity, or you can establish an equity line of credit.

To refinance the property, meet with your HOLD mortgage professional and see if your current equity position would allow you to pull out money in a refinance situation. Lenders generally want you to have a minimum of 30 percent equity remaining in the property, so you can only pull out a portion of the value to reinvest elsewhere. You can take out a line of credit against that equity. Lines of credit are useful because they not only allow you to take money from an existing investment and apply it to a new property, but also you generally only pay interest in the month or months you actually use the money so you can spread the loan out. For instance, instead of applying for a loan for $25,000 at your bank, a homeowner with a $25,000 line of credit can take out a $5,000 loan in April, a $10,000 loan in August, and a $10,000 loan in December, all with prior approval from the lender. By using a line of credit, you can take out just enough money to fund a specific property expense, then pay it back entirely before taking out additional funds.

That being said, the amount of interest charged for each smaller loan in a line of credit can be affected by an upward or downward change in the prime lending rate or other factors. Banks can also charge penalty fees for late payments on all outstanding loans, so you'll need to keep track of your individual loan obligations and work closely with your HOLD team, including your CPA.

Remember Jim and Linda's case, where they started acquiring and paying down more than they originally set out to and on a shorter time table? They looked at their portfolio and realized they had a tremendous amount of equity in their properties. So they obtained a line of credit with the bank taking second liens on the equity in their properties, and they used the money to purchase additional properties. This is a great way to leverage current investments to grow your portfolio, and if you work with your CPA, it's easy to manage.

2. Repurpose Your Existing Properties

Of course, taking out a line of credit on a property is not always the best decision. There are many ways to repurpose properties to their highest value. As one of our investor friends says: "Don't get caught up on the bricks and mortar of an individual investment." Just because you buy a single-family home doesn't mean that the property's greatest use is not as a commercial space. There are innumerable ways to utilize a property, and revisiting each of your investments on a regular basis will help you determine what's best for that specific lot. Here are a few ideas to get you started:

- **Single-family to multifamily**—If you're interested in upping your property's cash flow, look to see if there is a way to convert or add additional living space. For instance, if the current home sits on a large lot, consider adding a second "granny flat," and renting it as a duplex. Or, if there's no room for another building, see if you can build up rather than out, and include a separate entrance for the second floor apartment. We've even known people to install key locks on individual bedroom doors and rent each room to a separate tenant— usually students—with shared living spaces.

- **Subdivide**—Another option to consider on oversized lots is subdividing. We've had investor friends keep tabs on specific properties that have the option to subdivide. A strange thing happens when you divide things—the parts often turn out to be more valuable than the whole. Here's basically how it works: There is a small market of motivated buyers for large lots, which cost more money than smaller lots. How many people do you know that want or need a five-acre lot anyway? However, an investor might purchase that large five-acre lot for $500,000, and then, work to get a subdivision approved and have the property replatted. If successful, five one-acre lots might be created worth $125,000 each. They have a greater total value than the original lot. This is because the size is more attractive to a larger pool of buyers. Next time you drive through your subdivision, realize that at some time in the past an investor like you drove through what was then a pasture and had a vision that people would someday want to live there. They bought it, subdivided it, and either sold it to a developer or build on the lots themselves.

- **Residential to commercial**—Neighborhoods change, and what was once a quiet family street, might become a booming small business mecca over the course of ten years. Looking into your property's zoning and converting from residential to commercial can immediately add value.

Of course all of these options—as any repurpose would—require specific knowledge and permissions. It's important to keep your HOLD team involved and stay active in your investor networks to get the best possible leg up before moving ahead with any kind of repurpose.

3. Trade Up with a 1031 Exchange

If a repurpose isn't in your future but you'd still like to trade up or move from a single-family home to two duplexes, a 1031 exchange can be one of the most potent tools in your investment arsenal. Based on a provision in section 1031 of the U.S. tax code, a 1031 exchange allows a taxpayer to sell investment or business property and "exchange" it with like-kind replacement properties without having to pay federal income taxes on the transaction. Meaning? You can defer paying federal income taxes, continually trade up properties, and relocate your entire investment portfolio if you want to!

That being said, there are some rules that apply. For instance, the time you have to find an exchange property and then actually purchase is a very short window. There are other restrictions involved in a 1031 exchange, and that's why we always advise investors to use experts skilled in these types of transactions. It is too easy to make a mistake and lose your tax deferral. Not only that, the penalties for a disallowed exchange can be severe. The IRS can assess the back taxes owed with a 25 percent penalty, and 20 percent interest. Specifics such as these make 1031 exchanges more advanced than other options, but as an investor they are something you must know about, whether you decide to use them or not.

Let's look at an example to grasp the scope of savings with a 1031 exchange. Say your friend Billy sells a duplex for $450,000 that he has owned as an investment property for several years. He purchased it for $150,000. Assuming Billy paid $15,000 in capital improvements and the property depreciated $30,000, that leaves an adjusted basis of $135,000. Billy finds an apartment building—the replacement property—for $1.5 million. He purchases the property using the net proceeds from his duplex within the time period allotted, deferring his capital gains and depreciation recapture taxes. He now has $50,700 more to invest into a replacement property. Here's how the transaction would look:

Doing the Math on a 1031 Exchange	
Original Purchase Price	$150,000
+Capital Improvements	$15,000
-Depreciation	$30,000
Adjusted Basis	**$135,000**
Sale Price	$450,000
Sale Expenses (estimated 6 % of sale price)	$27,000
Net Sale Price	$423,000
Realized Gain (Net Sale – Adjusted Basis)	**$288,000**
Depreciation Recapture ($30,000 x 25%)	$ 7,500
Capital Gains Tax ($288,000 x 15%)	$ 43,200
Total Federal Taxes Amount	**$ 50,700**

Figure 16-1

The idea behind section 1031 is that when a property owner reinvests the sale proceeds from one property into another, the economic gain has not been realized in a way that generates funds to pay taxes. In other words, the taxpayer's investment is still the same, only the form has changed (e.g., vacant land exchanged for an apartment building). Therefore, it would be unfair to force the taxpayer to pay tax on a "paper" gain.

As long as the replacement property is held for investment, the 'like-kind' qualification can apply to any number of transactions, such as exchanging a rental property for land, an office building, warehouse, commercial property, or even a beach or mountain home. What's more, you can sell your property to one party and buy your replacement property from another, or sell one property and "exchange" it into two, three, or more replacements. Remember Steve's college-fund journey?

Just remember, as lucrative and rewarding as a 1031 exchange can be, they are also more advanced and carry some strict stipulations. So, while you should be aware of them, it's important to make sure and discuss your plan to use one thoroughly with your HOLD investment team, especially your CPA. It's also not a bad idea to have a few exchange properties in mind before entertaining the idea to make sure you meet deal deadlines.

POINTS TO REMEMBER

- It might not be one investment property that sustains you over time.

- The further along you get on your HOLD journey, the more opportunities will present themselves and the bigger your goals may get.

- There are many, many options and strategies to find, fund, and leverage new or existing investments.

- Be sure to have a clear plan and stick with it.

- Some models will be market specific. Do your due diligence and consult your HOLD team before entering into unchartered territory.

PUTTING IT ALL TOGETHER

When we are dreaming alone it is only a dream. When we are dreaming with others, it is the beginning of reality.

DOM HELDER CAMARA

Think back to when you first saw or heard about this book and decided to buy it. What was your motivation then? Maybe you wanted greater control of your time and you thought that successful real estate investing could provide it. Maybe you saw real estate investing as a long-term, lifelong path to freedom, riches, or security. Or maybe you simply desired a better life for yourself and the people you love. Like many successful real estate investors before you, at the beginning of this journey, you were probably thinking about changing your life to make it more fulfilling.

That time is now.

We've walked you through the hypothetical Springfield HOLD story. You found two prospects, analyzed both to make sure they fit your criteria, made your offers, stuck to your goals to eliminate one, purchased your first investment property, and managed respectable tenants for year one. Now it's time to grow, and for you, that means taking all you've learned from 742 Evergreen Terrace and applying it to your own HOLD journey. As Gary Keller said in *The Millionaire Real Estate Investor*: "Anyone can do it, not everyone will ... will you?" We hope your answer is yes, because we know that you can. How? Because we've done it. You just need to take the first step.

As the authors of this book, we'll be the first to tell you we weren't smarter or more skilled than anyone else when we started out. We didn't have the benefit of wealth or the right connections. Steve was a young man from New York who moved out West looking for broader horizons. Jennice was a property manager who never thought about owning her own properties. And Jim and Linda were starting over after a failed business left them with a mountain of debt and a resolve to create a secure financial future. Yet, through our individual journeys of becoming real estate investors, we've each found great financial, professional, and personal rewards. We opened one door and we didn't stop there.

As you follow the path of buying and HOLDing real estate, you will make some profound discoveries. First, you will experience the challenges and joys of achieving your goals. Second, you will find out that it was easier than you thought it would be. Third, you might find that when the people around you start looking at what you accomplished, they'll be inspired to come along and create even more opportunities—we certainly did.

This is actually one of our reasons for writing this book. By sharing the accumulated wisdom of successful HOLD investors and giving you a proven, workable plan to follow, you now have the knowledge you need to take that first step and the courage to say "Yes!" to your dreams.

1. Be an investor, not a speculator.

Benjamin Graham, the legendary American economist and professional investor, once described speculation as "a rat race of trying to get the highest possible return in the shortest period of time." Investors on the other hand, adhere to their investment strategies, do what works over and over again, do not take on unnecessary risk, and only venture into uncharted investment areas after careful investigation. Don't buy on speculation. If you can't sell a property tomorrow for more than you bought it for today, don't buy it.

2. Cash flow is king.

We've said it all along the HOLD journey, but we'll say it one more time: cash flow is king. A property that pays for itself never has to go up in value—even though most will. Always stick to your criteria, and your journey will be almost impossible to poke holes in.

3. It isn't personal, and the numbers matter most.

The biggest mistake people make when buying an investment property is to let emotion cloud good judgment. They buy a property because they like it—even when the numbers don't make sense. In order for any real estate investment to succeed, the numbers must make sense. Period.

4. Learn the magic of leverage.

Leverage is one of the most powerful and promising aspects of real estate. We don't know of another investment opportunity that you can buy at 25 cents on the dollar at a fixed rate of interest over a long period of time. That's how you leverage money. You leverage your investment by buying right—at least 10 percent below market value—so you make money from the day you close. You can then use your equity gains to increase your cash flow or fund other investments.

5. Cultivate relationships.

Surround yourself with smart people. Reach out to knowledge leaders and experienced investors. Associate with people who know more than you do and listen well. Instead of just asking, "What do I need to do?" turn the question around and say, "Who can I talk to?" As soon as you change the question from "what" to "who," you'll be surprised how many people show up to help you. These mentors will not only save you time and money, they will also teach you things quickly that otherwise may take many years to learn. Build your personal investment team of professionals who understand your investment strategy—they'll make your life easier and you'll increase the speed of new opportunities when you bring their energies together.

6. Keep learning.

All the successful investors we know continue to read books, listen to tapes, and attend seminars, looking for something to expand their knowledge or solve a problem. You can always learn something new, no matter how long you've been in the game. People who focus on learning and growth are the people best positioned to recognize opportunities.

7. Give to others.

The most successful people we know are usually the ones that are the most generous with their time. It's one of the universal laws of abundance: the more you give, the more you get—whether it be knowledge, opportunities, friendship, love, money, or other material rewards. Pay back the people who have helped you on your journey by helping other investors starting theirs.